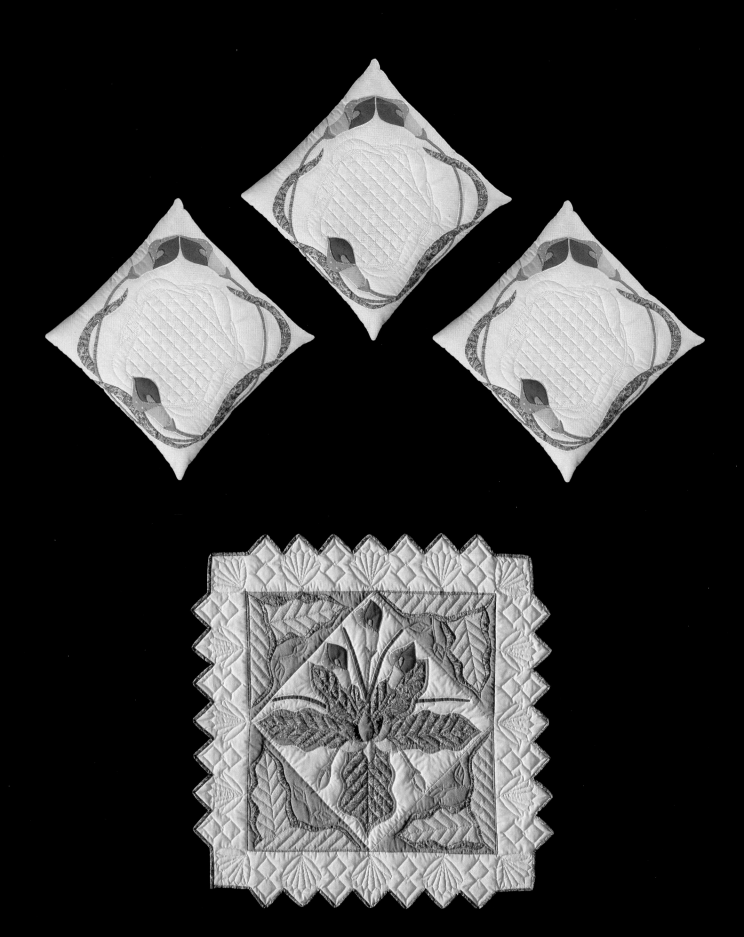

The Country Lily Quilt

The
Country Lily
Quilt

Cheryl A. Benner
and
Rachel T. Pellman

also
"The Country Lily Nine-Patch Variation Quilt"

Good Books
Intercourse, Pennsylvania 17534

Acknowledgments
Design by Cheryl A. Benner
Cover and color photography by Jonathan Charles
Author photo by Kenneth Pellman

The Country Lily Quilt
© 1990 by Good Books, Intercourse, PA 17534
International Standard Book Number:
0-934672-88-1
Library of Congress Catalog Card Number:
90-3078

Library of Congress Cataloging-in-Publication Data

Benner, Cheryl A., 1962–
   The country lily quilt.

   1. Quilting—Patterns   I. Pellman, Rachel T. (Rachel
Thomas)   II. Title.
TT835.B34   1990   746.46—dc20   90-3078
ISBN 0-934672-88-1

Table of Contents

The
Country Lily
Quilt

The Country Lily quilt offers a fresh new design for lovers of applique quilts. In place of the more commonly used tulip, daisy and rose motifs, the Country Lily follows the sophisticated and graceful lines of the Calla Lily. The lily flower is set among two types of leaves—one large and full-bodied, the other slender and delicate.

The Country Lily uses five applique patches. These patches are set on an angle, creating triangular patches at each side and corner. The center patch is filled with stately lilies and leaves. The four surrounding patches contain a graceful appliqued lily wreath. Each triangular patch holds a pair of large leaves or a trio of lilies. The entire composition creates an image of delicate flowers protected by lush foliage.

Lilies also line the borders of this quilt. Each appliqued flower is paired with slender leaves and sits at each point of the zig-zagged edge. Quilting stitches outline and accent the applique work on the borders and the quilt top.

Different arrangements of the applique blocks can greatly affect the overall visual image of the quilt. Along with the original design, we offer a Country Lily Variation. In this Variation, nine applique patches are used. Because these patches are set straight rather than angled, the triangular blocks are eliminated.

The Country Lily is also a beautiful wallhanging. A single patch used with triangular leaf patches and set in a border makes a stunning wall piece. Pillows made from a single patch serve as lovely accents.

We present the Country Lily in several color schemes. Its possibilities are as numerous and varied as its individual creators. Enjoy!

How to Begin

Read the following instructions thoroughly before beginning work on your quilt.

Wash all fabrics before cutting them. This process will both pre-shrink and test them for colorfastness. If the fabric is not colorfast after one washing, repeat the washings until the water remains clear or replace the cloth with another fabric. If fabrics are wrinkled after washing and drying, iron them before using them.

Fabrics suitable for quilting are generally lightweight, tightly woven cotton and cotton/polyester blends. They should not unravel easily and should not hold excessive wrinkles when squeezed and released. Because of the hours of time required to make a quilt, it is worth investing in high quality fabrics.

Fabric requirements given here are for standard 45″ wide fabric. If you use wider or more narrow fabrics, calculate the variations you will need.

All seams are sewn using ¼″ seam allowances. Measurements given include seam allowances except for applique pieces (see "How to Applique" section).

Applique Quilts

Preparing Background Fabric for Appliqueing

When you purchase fabric for the background and borders, buy the total amount you need from one bolt of fabric. This will ensure that all the patches and borders will be the same shade. Dye lots can vary significantly from bolt to bolt of fabric, and those differences are emphasized when placed next to each other in a quilt top.

Cutting diagrams are shown to make the most efficient use of fabric. Label each piece after it is cut. Mark right and wrong sides of fabric as well.

So that you know where to place the applique pieces on the background piece, trace the applique design lightly on the right side of the background fabric before beginning to stitch. Even though the applique pieces will be laid over these markings and stitched in place, it is important to mark these lines as lightly as possible. Center the applique designs on the background sections. The placement of the applique on the pillow throw is an exception to that rule. Center that applique from side to side, but place it nearer the top of the quilt so that there is extra fullness for tucking the quilt under the pillows. The space from the top of the pillow throw section to the highest point of the applique design should measure about 10 inches.

Making Templates

Make templates from pattern pieces printed in this book, using material that will not wear along the edges from repeated tracing. Cardboard is suitable for pieces being traced only a few times. Plastic lids or the sides of plastic cartons work well for templates that will be used repeatedly. Quilt supply shops and art supply stores carry sheets of plastic that work well for template-making.

Quiltmaking demands precision. Remember that as you begin marking! First, test the template you have made against the original printed pattern for accuracy. The applique templates are given in their actual size, without seam allowances. Trace them that way. Then trace them on the right side of the fabric, but spaced far enough apart so that you can cut them approximately ¼″ outside the marked lines. The traced line is the fold line, indicating the exact shape of the applique piece. Since these lines will be on the right side of the fabric and will be on the folded edge, make the markings as light as possible.

Each applique piece needs to be traced separately (rather than having the fabric doubled), so the fold line is marked on each one. Note, too, that since some of the pieces face in opposite directions, some will need to be traced pointing in one direction and some will need to be traced pointing the opposite way (see illustration).

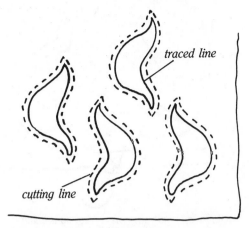

Applique templates should be traced on the right side of the fabric but spaced far enough apart so they can be cut approximately ¼″ outside the marked line.

Appliqueing

Begin by appliqueing the cut-out fabric pieces, one at a time, over the placement lines drawn onto the background fabric pieces. Be alert to the sequence in which the pieces are applied, so that sections which overlap each other are done in proper order. For example, when you do the center patch of the Country Lily quilt, you will need to do the leaves first. Lilies overlay leaves. In cases where a portion of an applique piece is covered by another, the section being covered does not need to be stitched, since it will be held in place by the stitches of the section that lies over it.

Appliqueing is not difficult, but it does require patience and precision. The best applique work has perfectly smooth curves and sharply defined points. To achieve this, stitches must be very small and tight. First, pin the piece being appliqued to the outline on the background piece. Using thread that matches the piece being applied, stitch the piece to the background section, folding the seam allowance under to the traced line on the applique piece. Fold under only a tiny section at a time.

The applique stitch is a running stitch going through the background fabric and emerging to catch only a few threads of the appliqued piece along the folded line. Make your needle re-enter the background piece for the next stitch at almost the same place it emerged, creating a stitch so small that it is almost invisible along the edge of the appliqued piece. Stitches on the underside of the background fabric should be about ⅛″ long.

To form sharp points, fold in one side and stitch almost to the end of the point. Fold in the opposite side to form the point and push the excess seam allowance under the point of the needle. You may trim the excess seam allowance to eliminate bulk. Stitch tightly.

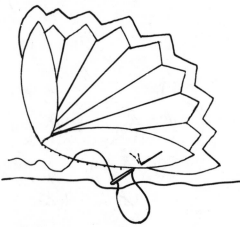

The applique stitch is a tiny, tight stitch that goes through the background fabric and emerges to catch only a few threads of the appliqued piece along the fold line.

Quilting lines are marked on the surface of the quilt top. Markings should be as light as possible so they are easily seen for quilting, yet do not distract when the quilting is completed.

To form smooth curves, clip along the curves to the fold line. Fold under while stitching, using the needle to push under the seam allowances.

Assembling the Appliqued Quilt Top

When all your applique work is completed, you are ready to assemble the patches. See the diagram on page 13. You can do most of the applique work on the borders before you assemble the quilt top. However, you will need to do the applique work on the corners after the top is assembled.

Quilting on Applique and Pieced Quilts
Marking Quilting Designs

Quilting designs are marked on the surface of the quilt top. A lead pencil provides a thin line and, if used with very little pressure, creates markings that are easily seen for quilting, yet do not distract when the quilt is completed. There are numerous marking pencils on the market, as well as chalk markers. Test whatever you choose on a scrap piece of fabric to be sure it performs as promised. Remember, quilting lines are not obliterated by quilting stitches, so make the lines light or removable.

Patterns for quilting designs are included in this book. Since most spread over several pages, you will need to assemble them before using them.

Quilting

A quilt consists of three layers—the back or underside of the quilt, the batting and the top, which is the appliqued layer. Quilting stitches follow a decorative pattern, piercing through all three layers of the quilt "sandwich" and holding it together.

Many quilters prefer to stretch their quilts into large quilting frames. These are built so that the finished area of the quilt can be rolled up as work on it progresses. This type of frame allows space for several quilters to work on the same quilt and is used at quilting bees. Smaller hoops can be used to quilt small sections at a time. If you use one of the smaller frames, it is important that you first stretch the three layers of the quilt in the frame, then baste them securely together to prevent puckering.

The quilting stitch is a simple running stitch. Quilting needles are called "betweens" and are shorter than "sharps," which are regular hand sewing needles. The higher the number, the smaller the needle. Many quilters prefer a size 8 or 9 needle.

Quilting is done with a single strand of quilting thread. Knot the thread and insert the needle through the top layer, about one inch away from the point where quilting should emerge on a marked quilting line. Gently tug the knot through the fabric so it is hidden between the layers. Then bring the needle up through the quilt top, going through all layers of the quilt.

Keep one hand under the quilt to feel when the needle has successfully penetrated all layers and to help guide the needle back up to the surface. Your upper hand receives the needle and repeats the process. It is possible to stack as many as five stitches on the needle before pulling the thread through. However, when you work curves, you have smoother results if you stack fewer stitches. Pull the quilting stitches taut but not so tight as to pucker the fabric. When you have used the entire length of thread, reinforce the stitching with a tiny backstitch. Then reinsert the needle in the top layer, push it through for a long stitch, pull it out and clip it.

The goal in quilting is to have straight, even stitches that are of equal length on both the top and bottom of the quilt. That achievement comes with hours of practice!

When you quilt the applique patches, simply outline the applique designs. This outline quilting will accent the applique section and cause it to appear slightly puffed.

A quilt is a sandwich of three layers—the quilt back, batting and the quilt top—all held together by the quilting stitches.

Binding

The final stage in completing a quilt is the binding, which finishes the quilt's raw edge. When binding a non-straight-edged quilt, cut the binding strips on the bias. This allows more flex and stretch around curves. To cut on the bias, cut the fabric at a 45 degree angle to the straight of grain.

A double thickness of binding on the edge of the quilt gives it additional strength and durability. To create a double binding, cut the binding strips 2–2½" wide. Sew strips together to form a continuous length of binding.

When binding a quilt with zig-zag edges, it is easier to attach the binding *before* cutting the zig-zag edge. To do so baste the raw edges of the quilt together. Mark but do not cut the jagged border. Using a ¼" seam allowance, sew the binding along the marked edge, pivoting at the end of each point to create a sharp turn. Trim the zig-zags even with the edge of the binding. Wrap the binding around to the back, enclosing the raw edges and covering the stitch line. Slipstitch in place with thread that matches the color of the binding fabric.

To Display Quilts

Wall quilts can be hung in various ways. You can simply tack the quilt directly to the wall. However, this is potentially damaging to both quilt and wall. Except for a permanent hanging, this is probably not the best way.

Another option is to hang the quilt like a painting. To do this, make a narrow sleeve from matching fabric and handsew it to the upper edge of the quilt along the back. Insert a dowel rod through the sleeve and hang the rod by wire or nylon string.

The quilt can also be hung on a frame. This method requires velcro or fabric to be attached to the frame itself. If you choose velcro, staple one side to the frame. Handsew the opposite velcro on

Mitering Corners

Step 1

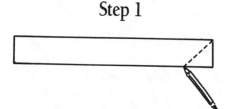

Measure in from each end the exact number of inches as the border width. Draw a diagonal line from that point to the outer corner. Cut along angled line.

Step 2

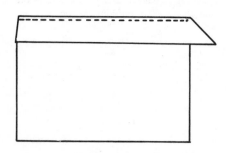

Stitch borders to quilt, leaving a ¼" seam allowance open at each mitered end.

Step 3

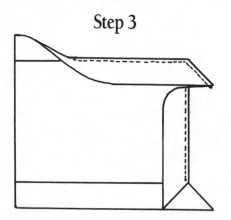

Stitch across the open ends of the corners from the inside corner to the outer edge.

the edges of the quilt, then attach the quilt carefully to the velcro on the frame. If you attach fabric to the frame, handstitch the quilt to the frame itself.

Quilts can also be mounted inside plexiglass by a professional framery. This method, often reserved for antique quilts, can provide an acid-free, dirt-free and, with special plexiglass, a sun-proof environment for your quilt.

Other Projects

The Country Lily pattern is adaptable to other projects as well. To make a wallhanging, follow the instructions for appliqueing but use only one square patch. This may be done as a single square like the patches of the Country Lily Variation. Add a border with decorative quilting and you have a lovely wallhanging.

For a larger wallhanging, tip the square patch on an angle as in the original design. Add a triangle with applique leaves on each corner to create a square. Surround this with a border and bind with a jagged edge or a straight edge. Borders on wallhangings may be mitered for a more tailored look. See the illustration for instructions on mitered corners.

Pillows can also be made using a single patch. The Lily Wreath patch would be a fine complement to the Country Lily wallhanging. Applique the pillow top and quilt the patch. To make the back of the pillow, cut a square equal in size to the front in either matching or contrasting fabric.

Make a ruffle using one of the fabrics used in the applique design. To make the ruffle, cut three strips of fabric measuring 4½" x 45" each. Sew these strips together to form a continuous length. Bring the two ends together, wrong sides together, and stitch to create a fabric circle. Fold the fabric circle in half with wrong sides together. Stitch along the raw edge with a long running stitch the entire circumference of the circle. Gather the circle to fit around the edges of the quilted top. Pin the ruffle to the pillow top with raw edges even, and spread the gathers evenly throughout. Baste the ruffle to the pillow top. With right sides together and the ruffle sandwiched between the layers, pin the back to the pillow top. Stitch back to top through all layers, leaving a five-inch opening along one side. Trim seams. Turn pillow right side out. Stuff pillow with polyester fiberfil. Slipstitch opening.

Signing and Dating Quilts

To preserve history for future generations, sign and date the quilts you make. Include your initials and the year the quilt was made. This data can be added discreetly in a corner of the quilt. Embroider or quilt it among the quilting designs. Another alternative is to stitch or write the information on a separate piece of fabric and handstitch it to the back of the quilt. Whatever method you choose, this is an important and lasting part of finishing a quilt.

The Country Lily Quilt
Cutting Lay-out for Queen-size or Double-size Quilt

Final size — approximately 93″ × 108″
Measurements include seam allowances

Total yardage for quilt top — 8⅜ yards
Total yardage for quilt back — 6¼ yards
plus 11″ remaining from cutting
borders of quilt top.

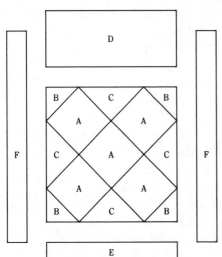

A Patches — cut 5 — 21½″ square
B Corner Triangles — 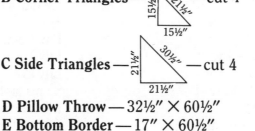 — cut 4
15½″ 21½″ 15½″

C Side Triangles — 21½″ 30½″ 21½″ — cut 4

D Pillow Throw — 32½″ × 60½″
E Bottom Border — 17″ × 60½″
F Side Borders — 17″ × 109″

Triangular Patches (1⅛ yards)
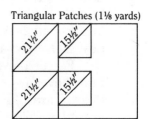
21½″ 15½″
21½″ 15½″

Side Borders (3⅛ yards)

Side Border — 17″ × 109″
Side Border — 17″ × 109″
Quilt Back — 11″ left

Quilt Back (6¼ yards) plus 11″ left from side border section of fabric

11″	45″	45″
11″ × 112″	45″ × 112″	45″ × 112″

Square Patches, Bottom Border, Pillow Throw (4⅛ yards)

	Bottom Border 17″ × 60½″		21½″
Pillow Throw 32½″ × 60½″	21½″	21½″ 21½″	21½″

Assembly Instructions for the Country Lily Quilt
Queen-size/Double-size

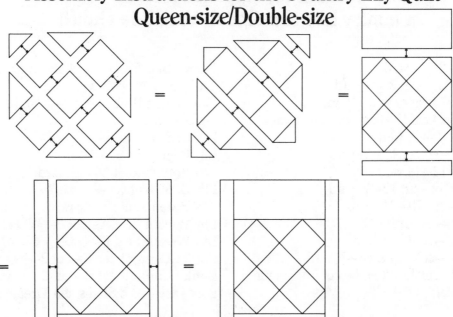

Yardage for Applique for the Country Lily Quilt

Leaf A—cut 6—⅓ yard
Leaf A Overlay—cut 6—⅓ yard
Leaf B—cut 10—⅓ yard
Leaf B Overlay—cut 10—⅓ yard
Leaf C—cut 4—¼ yard
Leaf C Overlay—cut 4—¼ yard
Leaf D—cut 2—⅛ yard
Leaf D Overlay—cut 2—⅛ yard
Leaf E—cut 2—¼ yard
Leaf E Overlay—cut 2—¼ yard
Leaf F—cut 1—¼ yard
Leaf F overlay—cut 1—¼ yard
Pillow Throw Leaf—cut 1—(Can be cut from same ¼ yard as Pillow Throw Leaf)
Pillow Throw Leaf Overlay—cut 1—(Can be cut from same ¼ yard as Pillow Throw Leaf)
Leaf—cut 6—⅛ yard
Flower Petal—cut 2—⅛ yard
Outer Petals—cut 2 of each—⅛ yard
Flower Bud—cut 4—(Can be cut from fabric for Lily Center)
Flower Bud Accent—cut 4—(Can be cut from fabric for Lily Bottom)
Flower Bud Base—cut 4—(Can be cut from fabric for Lily Base)
Spike Leaf—cut 66—1¼ yard
Lily Center—cut 59—¾ yard
Lily Edge—cut 59—⅞ yard
Lily Bottom—cut 59—⅓ yard—(Use bias tape for Stems and Wreath)
Lily Base—cut 59—⅛ yard
Lily Piston—cut 59—⅛ yard
Lily Wreath Leaf A—cut 8—⅔ yard
Lily Wreath Leaf B—cut 8—⅔ yard
Border Corner Leaf A—cut 2—(Can be cut from fabric left from Lily Wreath Leaf A and B)
Border Corner Leaf B—cut 2—(Can be cut from fabric left from Lily Wreath Leaf A and B)
Bias Tape—(For Stems and Wreaths)

Yardage for Applique for the Country Lily Nine-Patch Variation Quilt

Leaf A—cut 2—¼ yard
Leaf A Overlay—cut 2—¼ yard
Pillow Throw Leaf—cut 6—¼ yard
Pillow Throw Leaf Overlay—cut 6—¼ yard
Leaf C—cut 10—½ yard
Leaf C Overlay—cut 10—½ yard
Leaf B—cut 12—⅓ yard
Leaf B Overlay—cut 12—⅓ yard
Spike Leaf—cut 70—1⅓ yard
Leaf—cut 18—¼ yard
Flower Petal—cut 6—⅛ yard
Outer Petals—cut 6 of each—⅛ yard
Flower Bud—cut 12—(Can be cut from fabric for Lily Center)
Flower Bud Accent—cut 12—(Can be cut from fabric for Lily Bottom)
Flower Bud Base—cut 12—(Can be cut from fabric for Lily Base)
Lily Center—cut 65—1 yard
Lily Edge—cut 65—1 yard
Lily Bottom—cut 65—½ yard
Lily Base—cut 65—¼ yard
Lily Piston—cut 65—⅛ yard
Lily Wreath Leaf A—cut 8—⅔ yard
Lily Wreath Leaf B—cut 8—⅔ yard
Border Corner Leaf A—cut 2—⅔ yard
Border Corner Leaf B—cut 2—⅔ yard
Bias Tape—(For Stems and Wreaths)

Country Lily Quilt Applique Templates

3
Outer Petal

2
Outer Petal

1
Flower Petal

2
Outer Petal

3
Outer Petal

Leaf
(three per flower)

Lily Center

Lily Bottom

Lily Edge

Lily Piston

Lily Base

Note: Some lily templates will need to be cut facing the opposite direction.

A single completed lily will look like this:

15

Country Lily Quilt Applique Templates

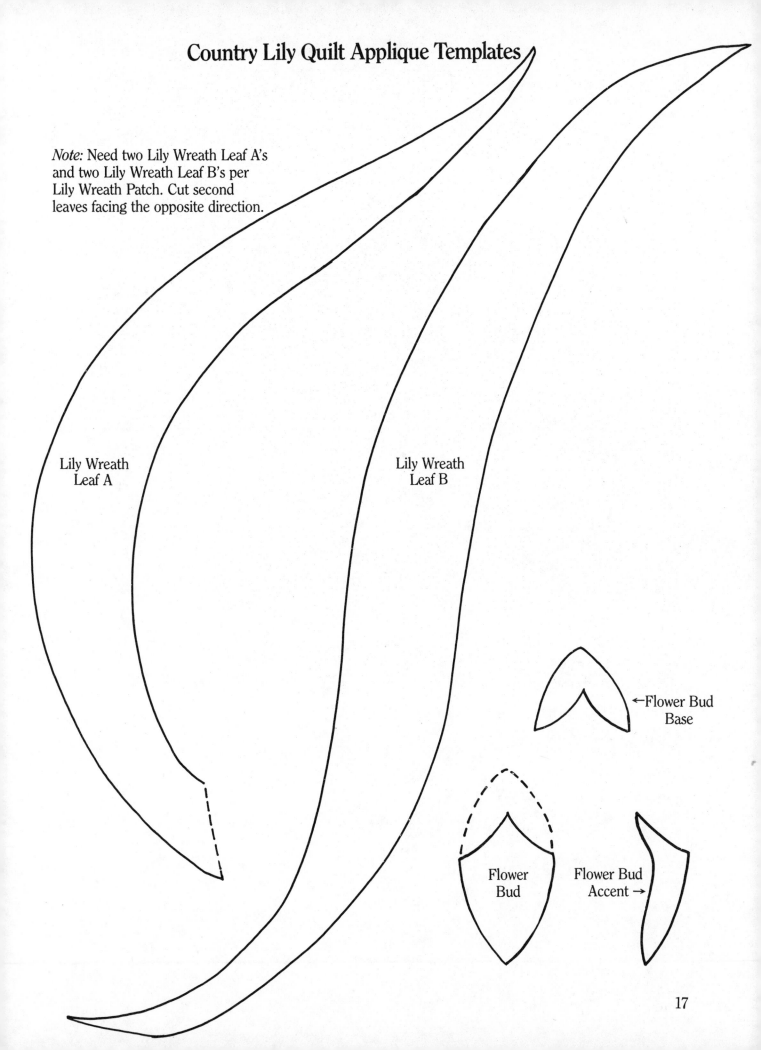

Note: Need two Lily Wreath Leaf A's and two Lily Wreath Leaf B's per Lily Wreath Patch. Cut second leaves facing the opposite direction.

Lily Wreath Leaf A

Lily Wreath Leaf B

←Flower Bud Base

Flower Bud

Flower Bud Accent →

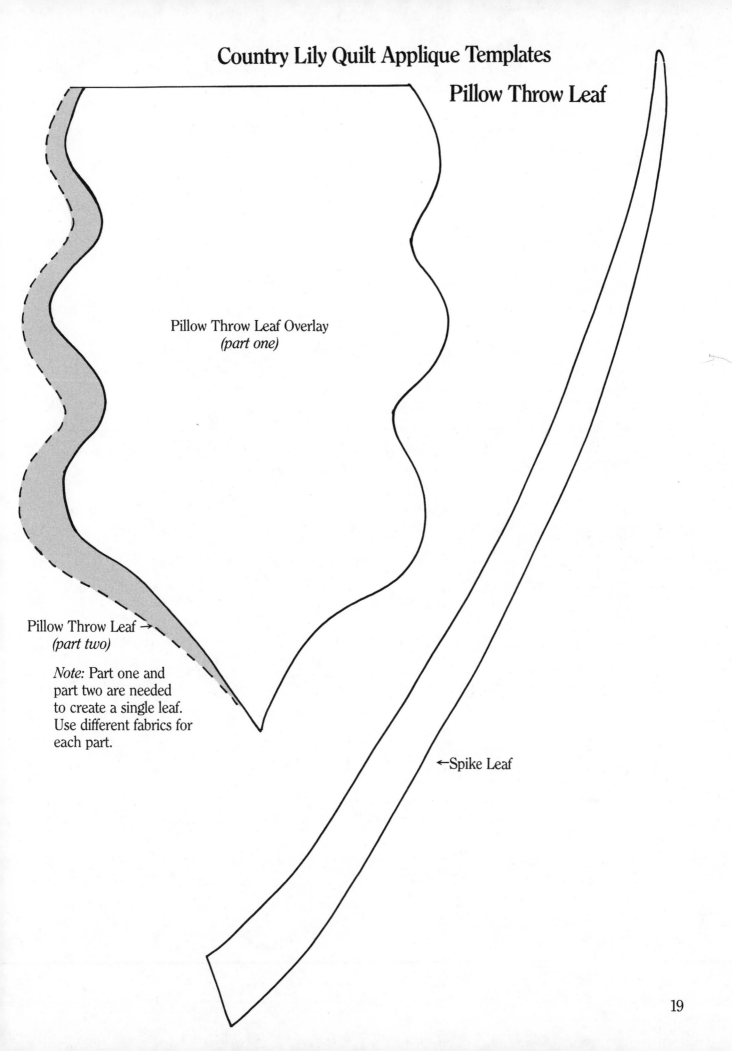

Country Lily Quilt Applique Templates

Pillow Throw Leaf

Pillow Throw Leaf Overlay
(part one)

Pillow Throw Leaf →
(part two)

Note: Part one and
part two are needed
to create a single leaf.
Use different fabrics for
each part.

←Spike Leaf

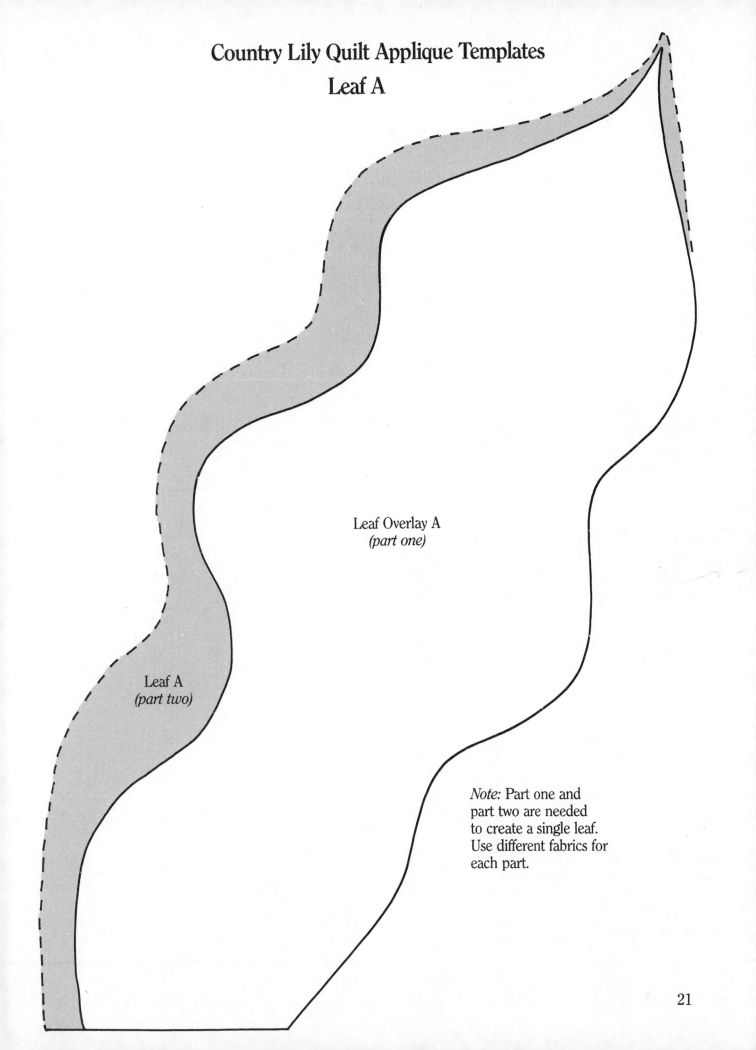

Country Lily Quilt Applique Templates
Leaf A

Leaf Overlay A
(part one)

Leaf A
(part two)

Note: Part one and part two are needed to create a single leaf. Use different fabrics for each part.

Country Lily Quilt Applique Templates
Leaf B

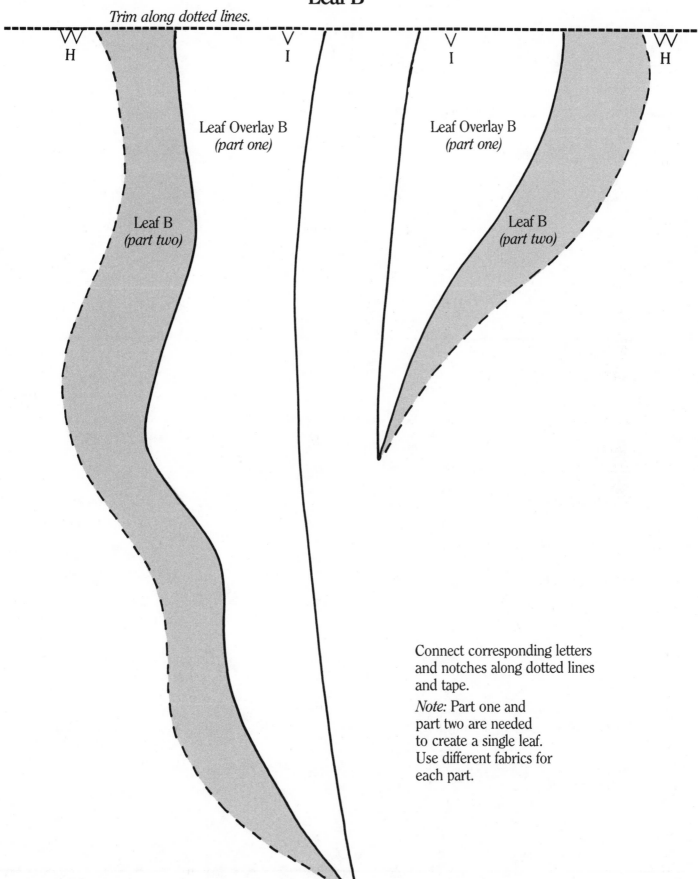

Trim along dotted lines.

H

V
I

V
I

H

Leaf Overlay B
(part one)

Leaf Overlay B
(part one)

Leaf B
(part two)

Leaf B
(part two)

Connect corresponding letters
and notches along dotted lines
and tape.

Note: Part one and
part two are needed
to create a single leaf.
Use different fabrics for
each part.

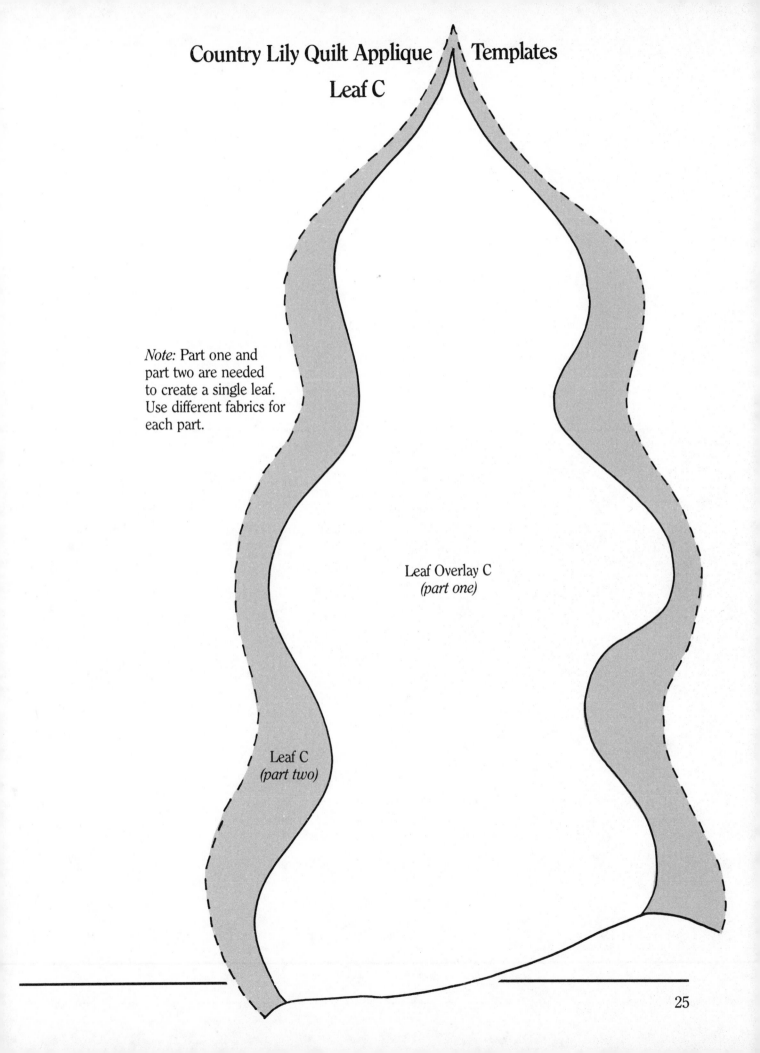

Country Lily Quilt Applique Templates
Leaf C

Note: Part one and part two are needed to create a single leaf. Use different fabrics for each part.

Leaf Overlay C
(part one)

Leaf C
(part two)

Country Lily Quilt Applique Templates
Leaf D

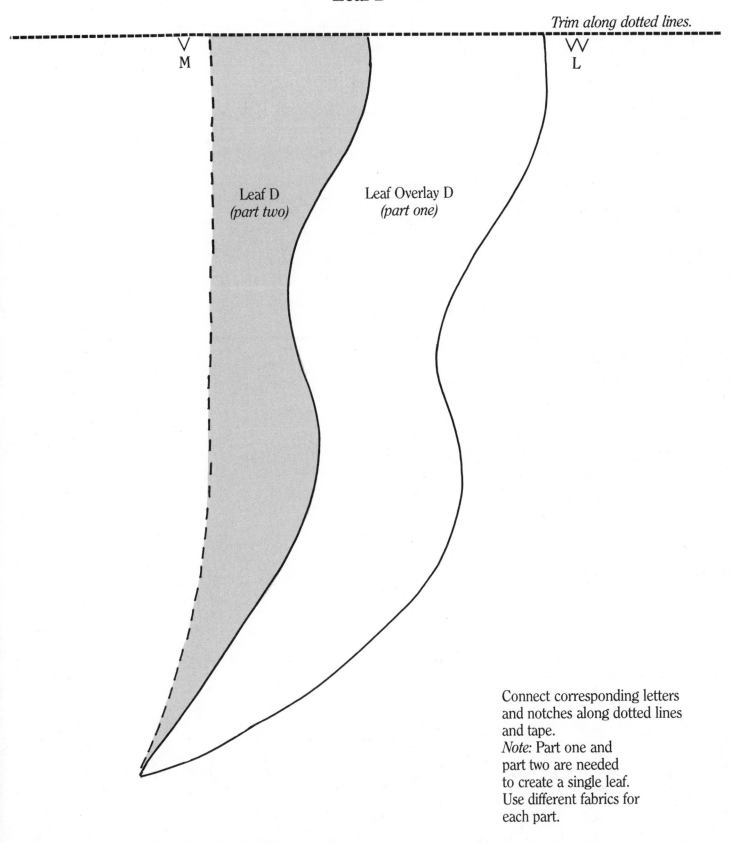

Trim along dotted lines.

M

L

Leaf D
(part two)

Leaf Overlay D
(part one)

Connect corresponding letters
and notches along dotted lines
and tape.
Note: Part one and
part two are needed
to create a single leaf.
Use different fabrics for
each part.

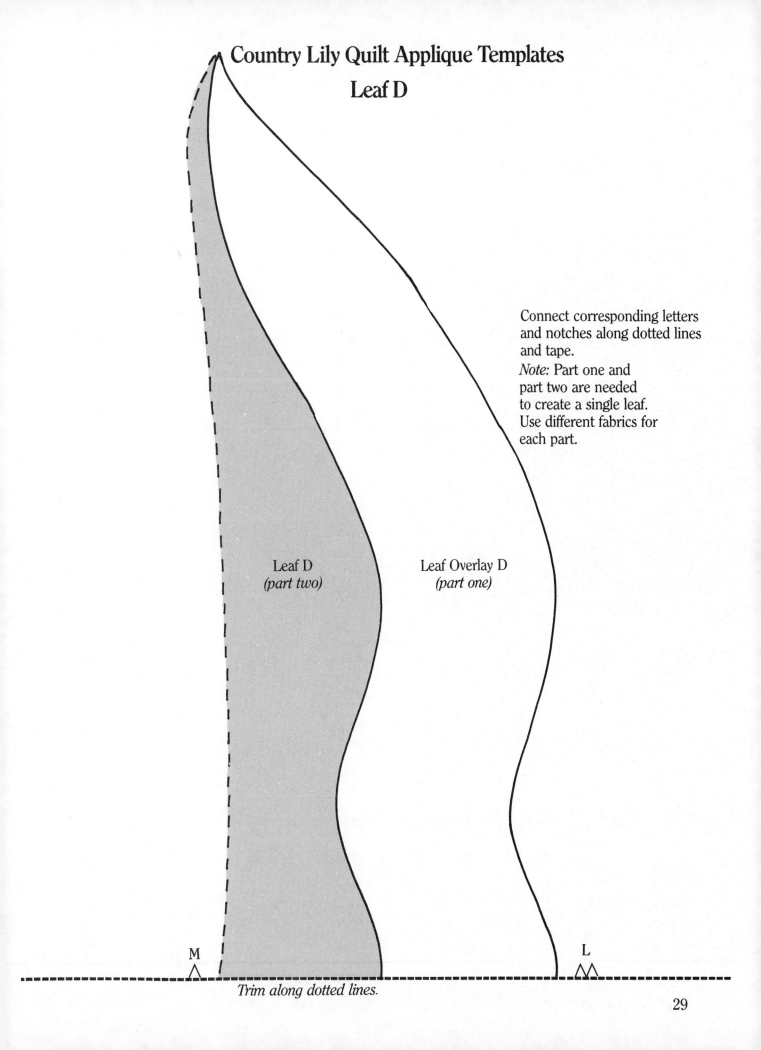

Country Lily Quilt Applique Templates
Leaf D

Connect corresponding letters
and notches along dotted lines
and tape.
Note: Part one and
part two are needed
to create a single leaf.
Use different fabrics for
each part.

Leaf D
(part two)

Leaf Overlay D
(part one)

M

L

Trim along dotted lines.

Country Lily Quilt Applique Templates

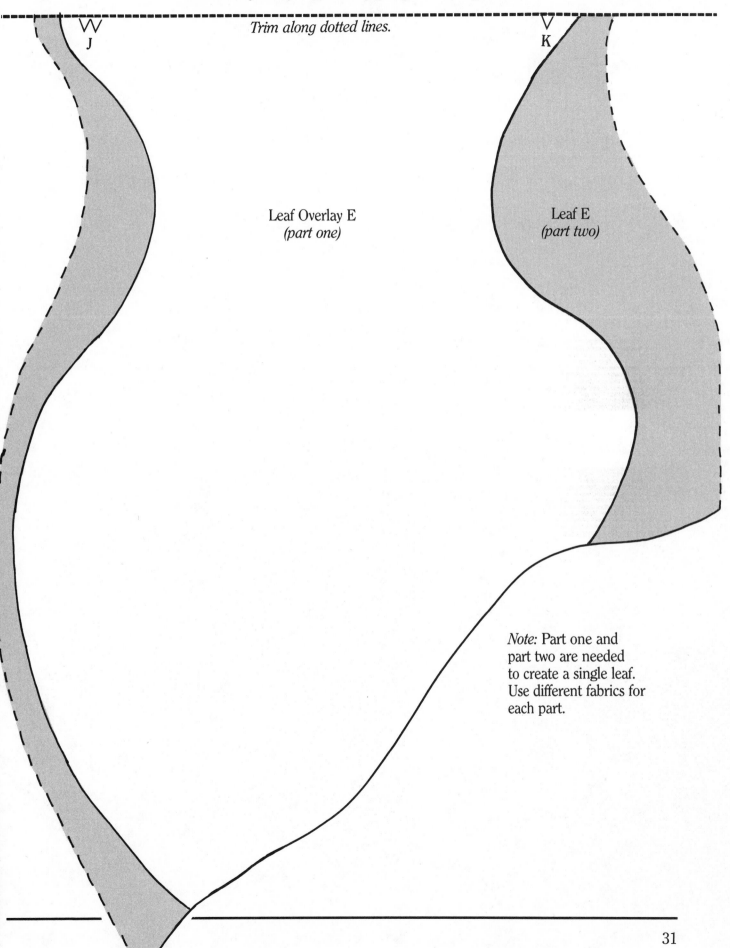

Trim along dotted lines.

J

Leaf Overlay E
(part one)

K

Leaf E
(part two)

Note: Part one and
part two are needed
to create a single leaf.
Use different fabrics for
each part.

Country Lily Quilt Applique Templates

Leaf E

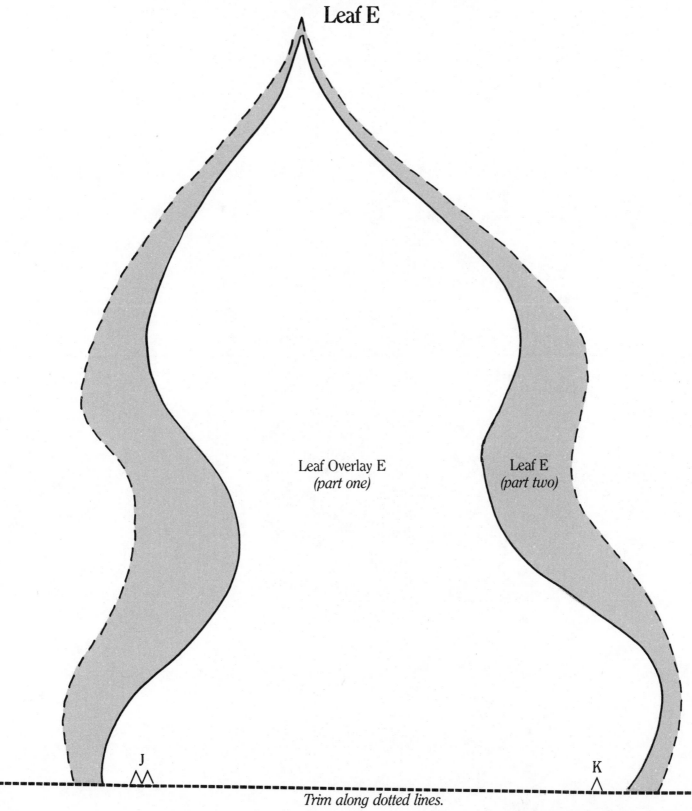

Leaf Overlay E
(part one)

Leaf E
(part two)

J

K

Trim along dotted lines.

Note: Part one and part two are needed to create a single leaf. Use different fabrics for each part.

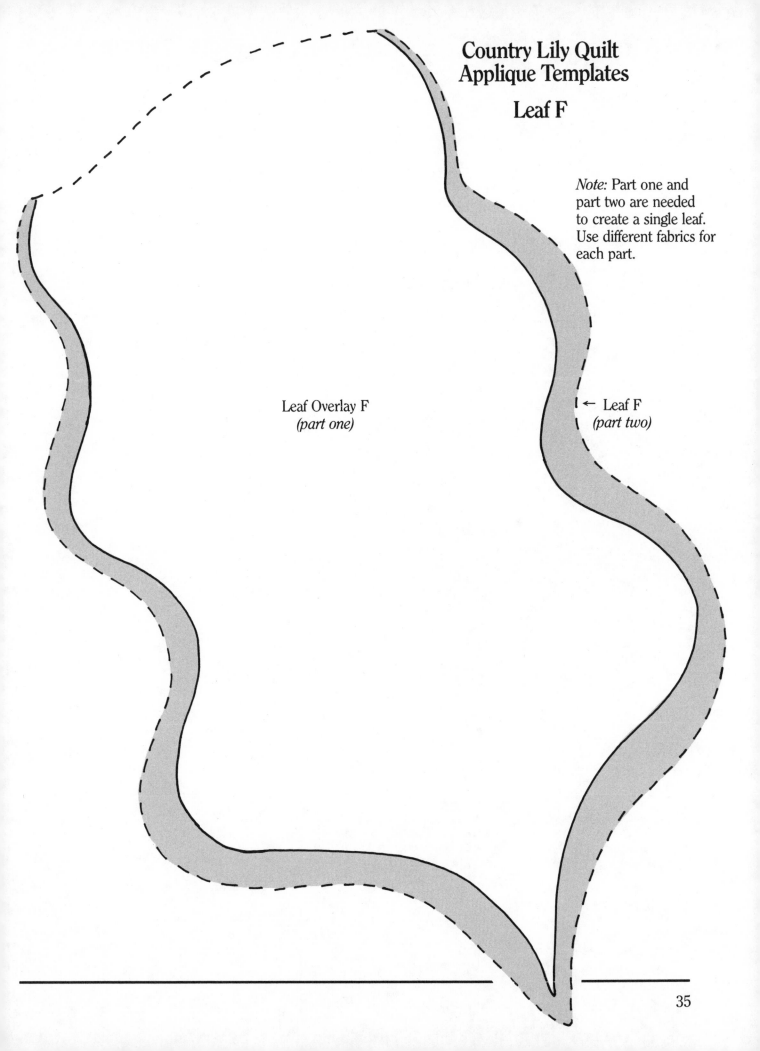

Country Lily Quilt
Applique Templates

Leaf F

Note: Part one and
part two are needed
to create a single leaf.
Use different fabrics for
each part.

Leaf Overlay F
(part one)

← Leaf F
(part two)

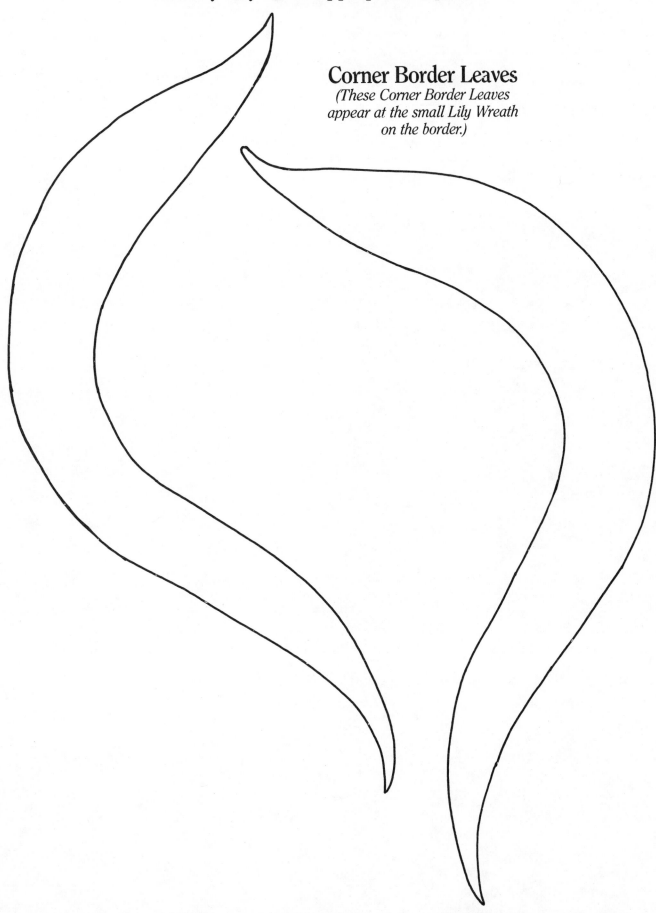

Corner Border Leaves
*(These Corner Border Leaves
appear at the small Lily Wreath
on the border.)*

Country Lily Quilt Applique Layout

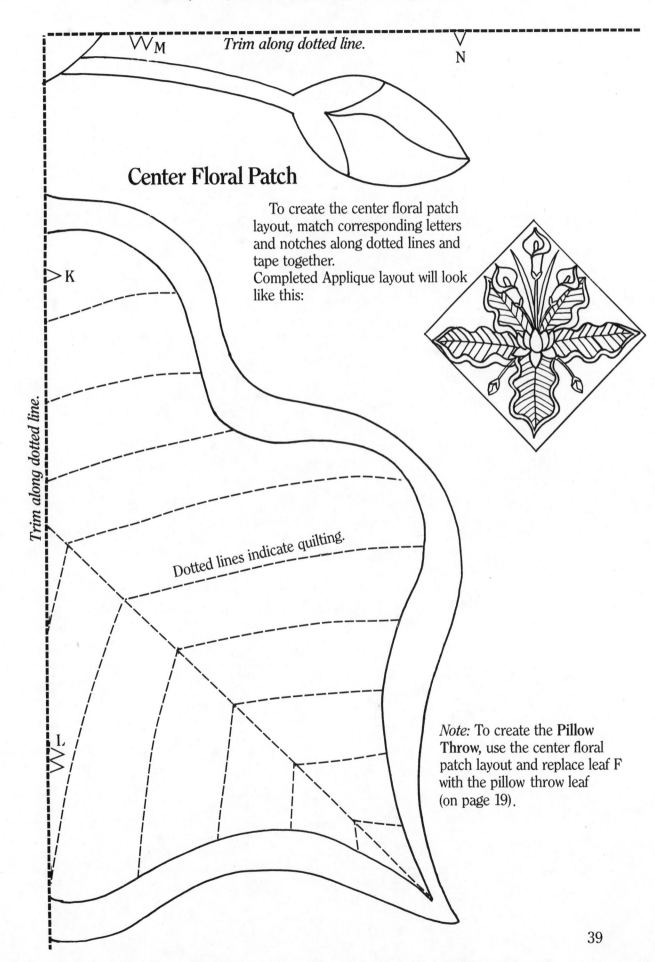

M

N

Center Floral Patch

To create the center floral patch layout, match corresponding letters and notches along dotted lines and tape together.
Completed Applique layout will look like this:

K

Trim along dotted line.

Dotted lines indicate quilting.

L

Note: To create the **Pillow Throw**, use the center floral patch layout and replace leaf F with the pillow throw leaf (on page 19).

Country Lily Quilt Applique Layout
Center Floral Patch

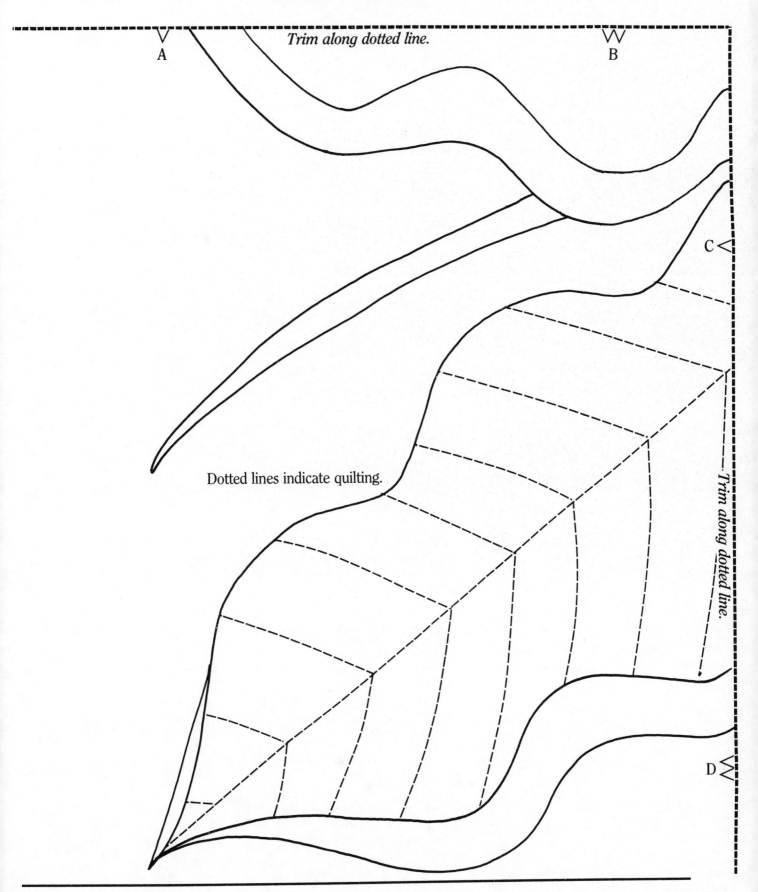

Trim along dotted line.

A

B

C

Dotted lines indicate quilting.

Trim along dotted line.

D

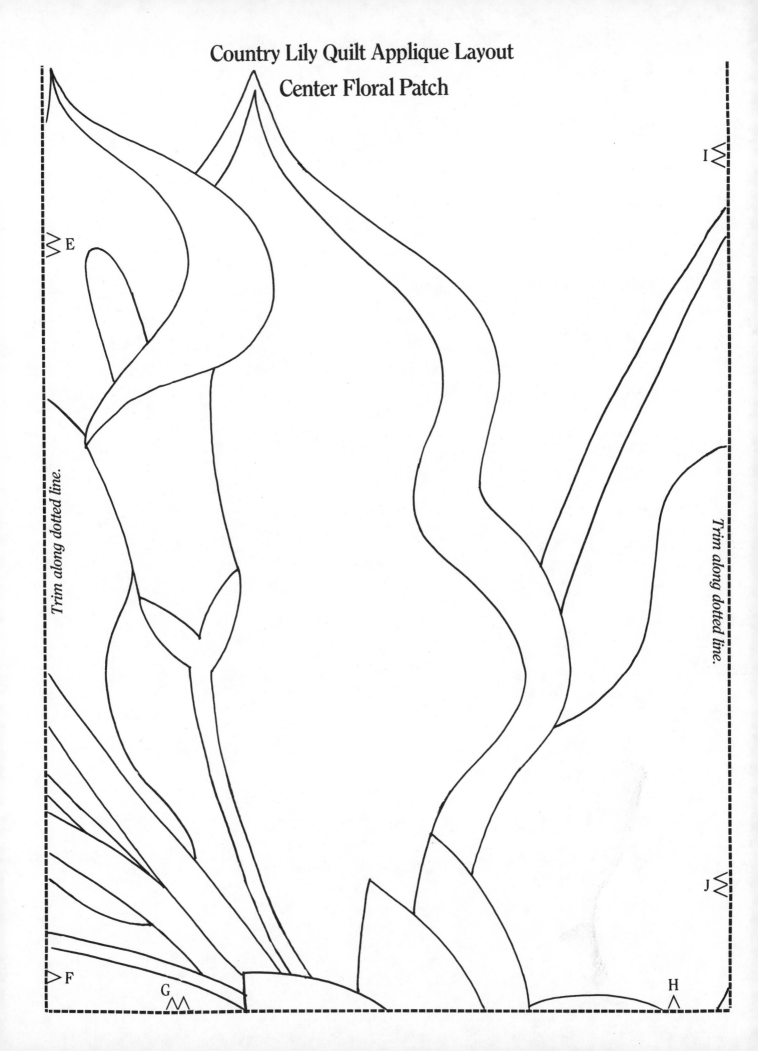

Country Lily Quilt Applique Layout
Center Floral Patch

Trim along dotted line.

Trim along dotted line.

E

I

F

G

H

J

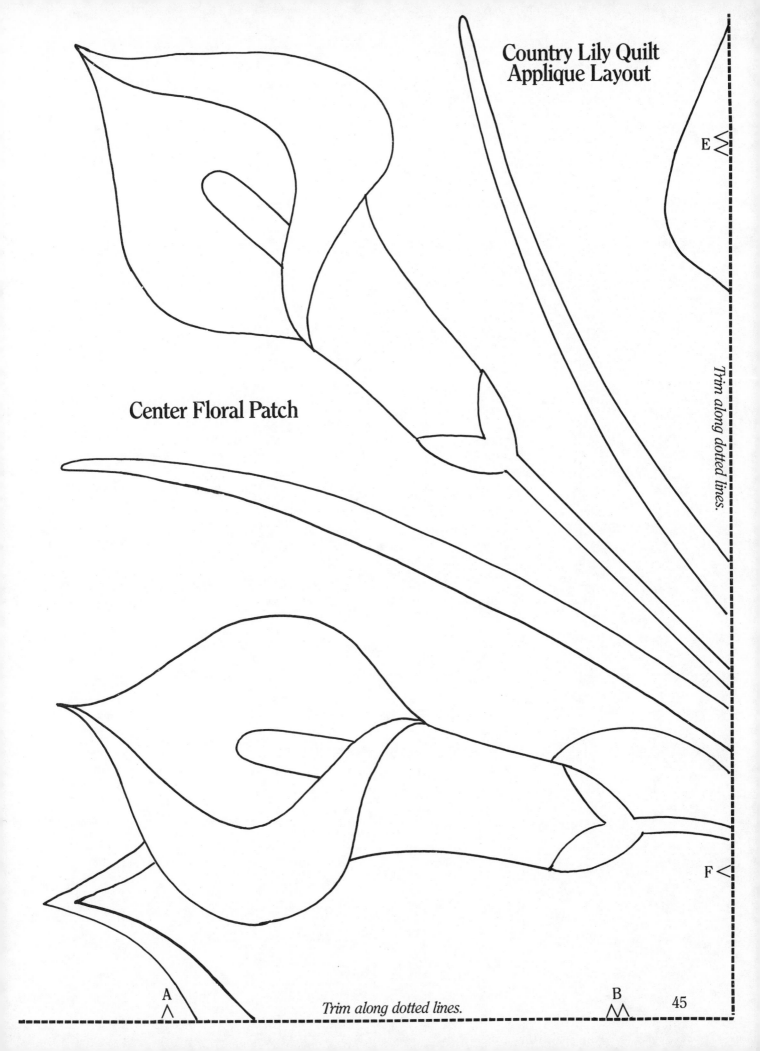

Country Lily Quilt
Applique Layout

E

Trim along dotted lines.

Center Floral Patch

F

A

Trim along dotted lines.

B

45

Country Lily Quilt Applique Layout

Center Floral Patch

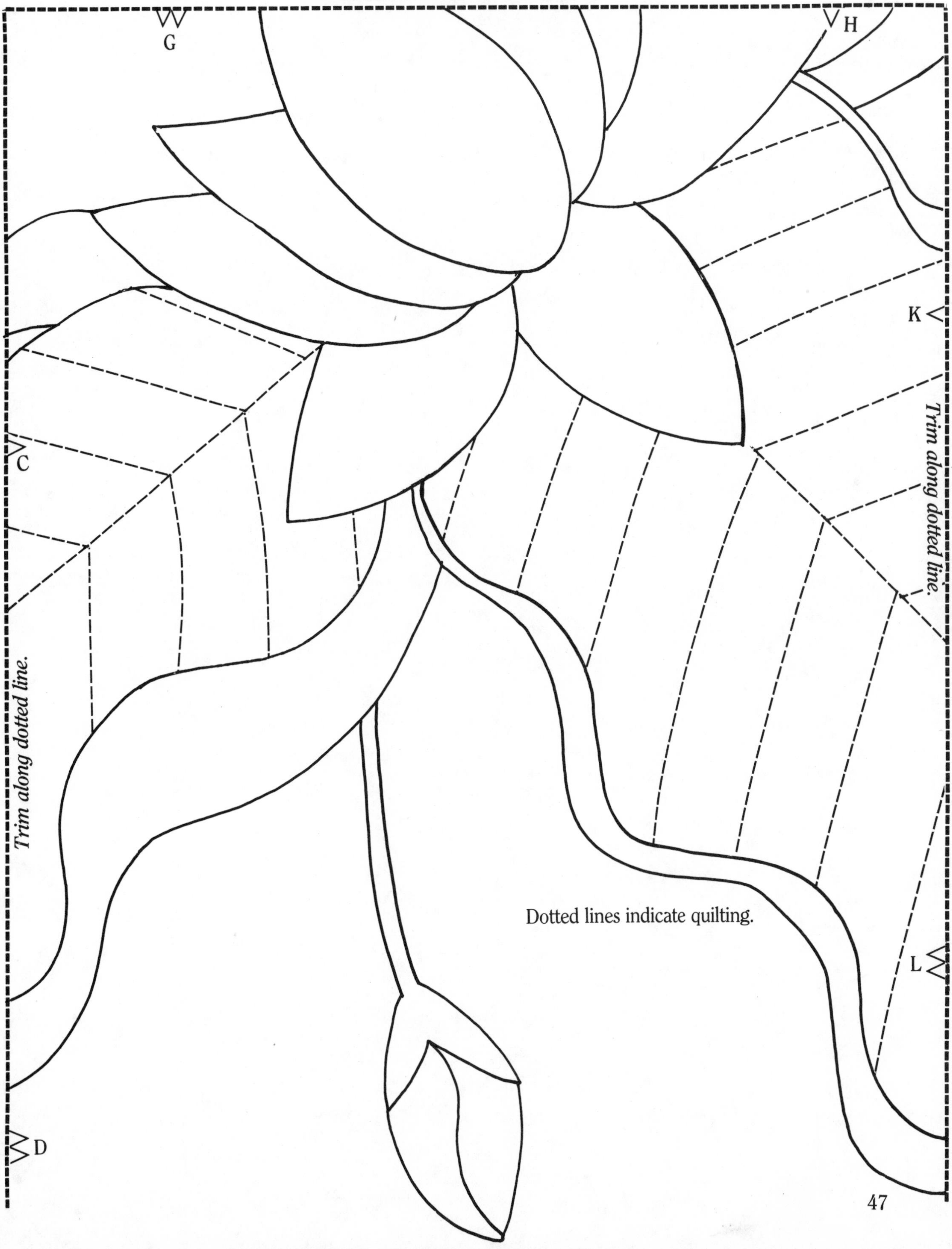
G
H
K
C
Trim along dotted line.
Trim along dotted line.
Dotted lines indicate quilting.
L
D

Country Lily Quilt Applique Layout
Center Floral Patch

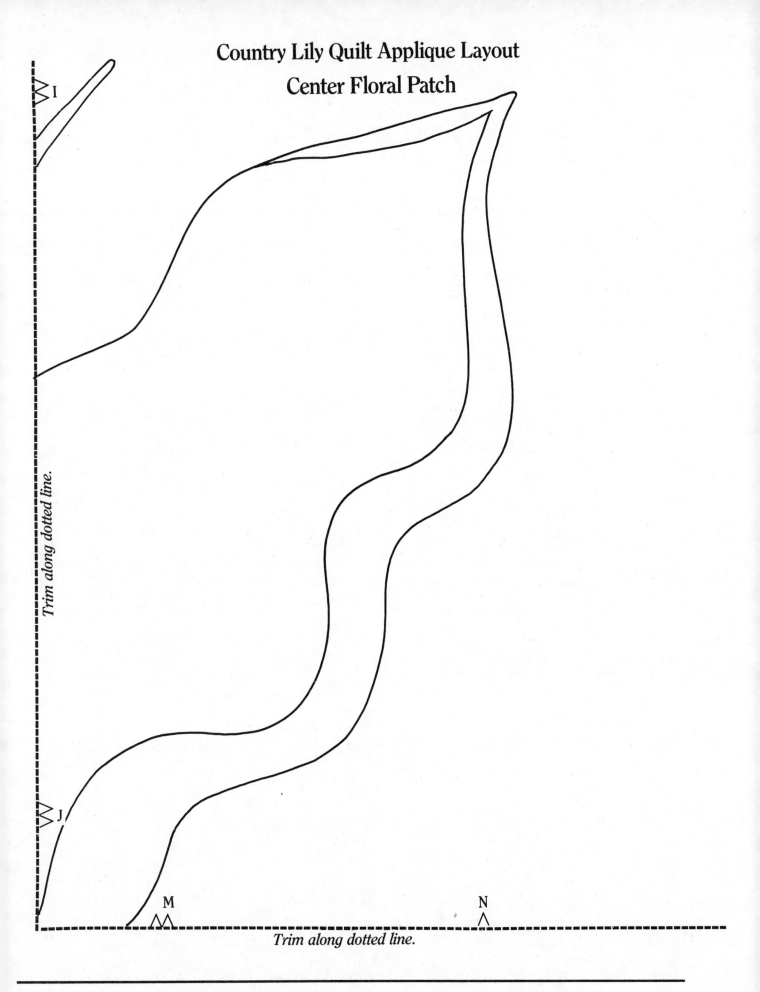

Country Lily Quilt Applique Layout
Lily Wreath Patch

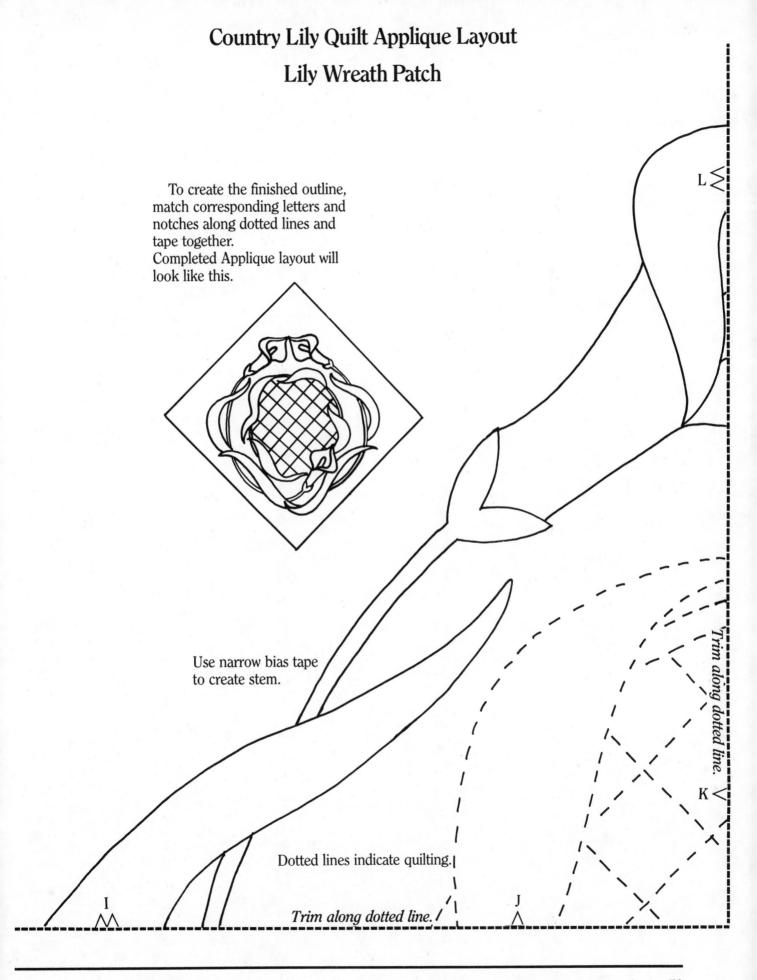

To create the finished outline, match corresponding letters and notches along dotted lines and tape together.
Completed Applique layout will look like this.

Use narrow bias tape to create stem.

L

Dotted lines indicate quilting.

Trim along dotted line.

I

Trim along dotted line.

K

J

Dotted lines indicate quilting.

Trim along dotted line.

Trim along dotted line.

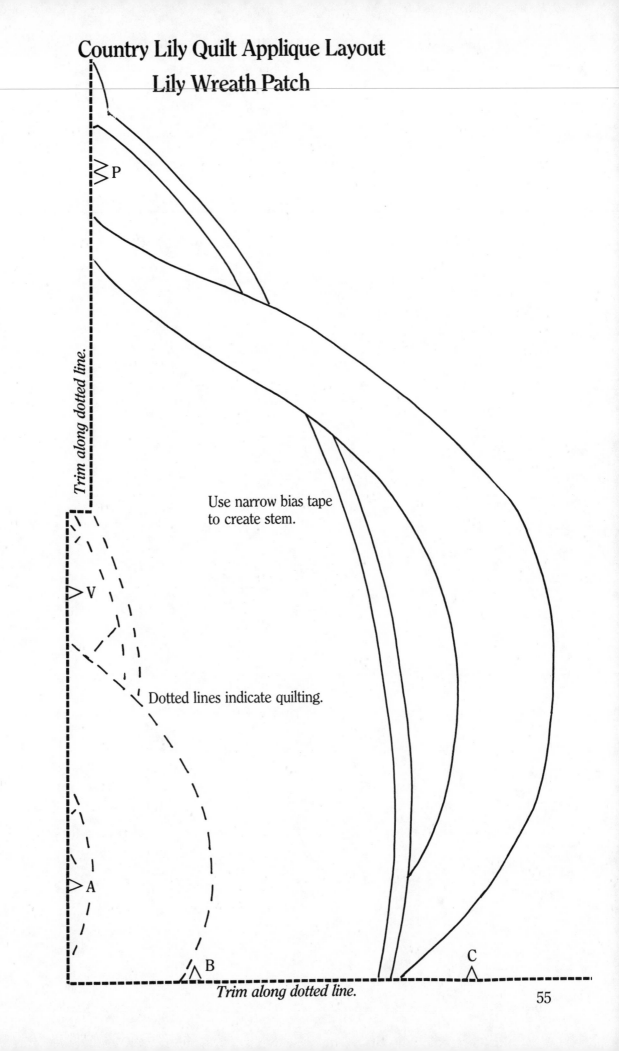

Country Lily Quilt Applique Layout
Lily Wreath Patch

Trim along dotted line.

P

Use narrow bias tape
to create stem.

V

Dotted lines indicate quilting.

A

B

C

Trim along dotted line.

55

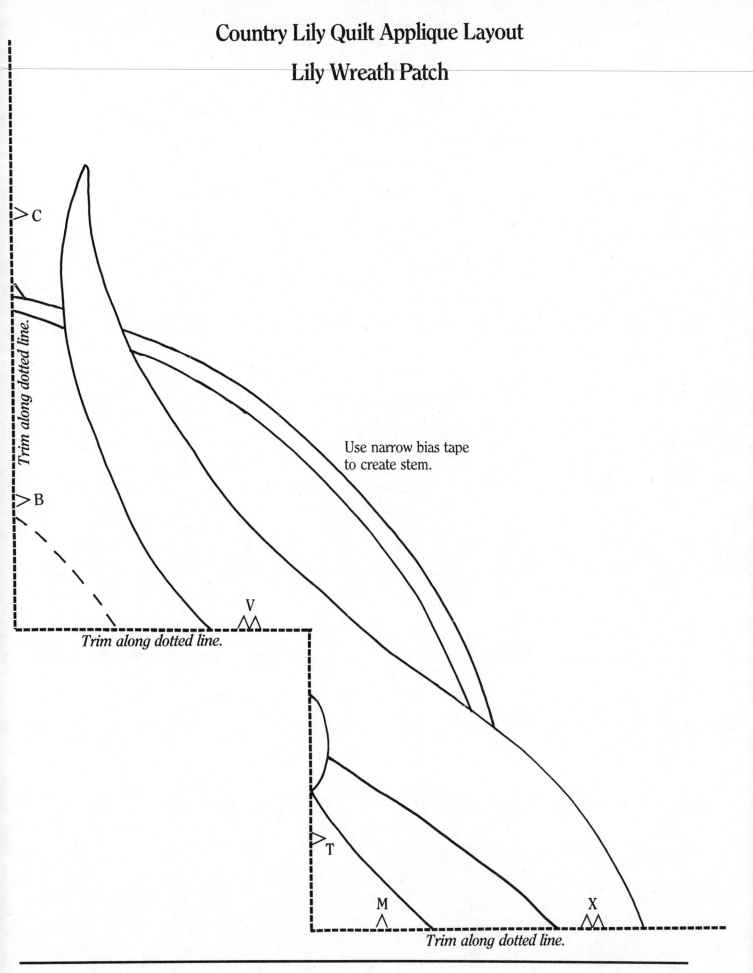

C

Trim along dotted line.

B

Use narrow bias tape
to create stem.

V

Trim along dotted line.

T

M

X

Trim along dotted line.

Dotted lines indicate quilting.

Trim along dotted line.

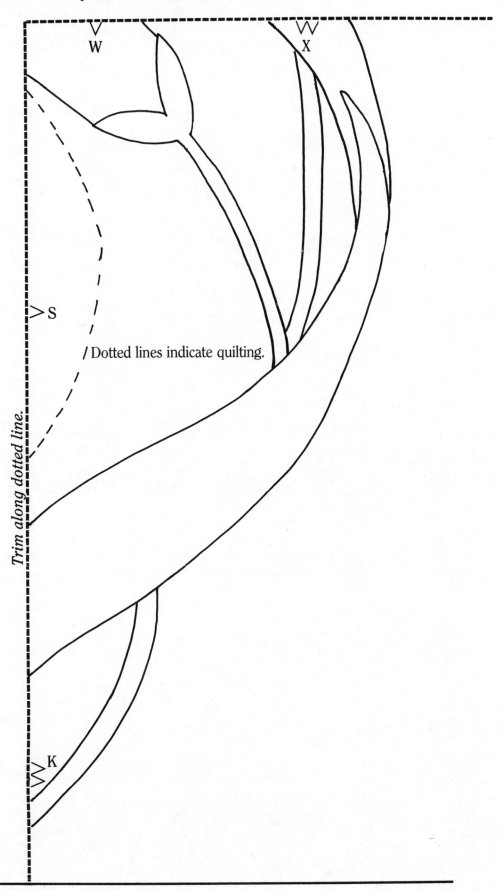

W

X

S

/ Dotted lines indicate quilting.

Trim along dotted line.

K

Country Lily Quilt Applique Layout

Lily Wreath Patch

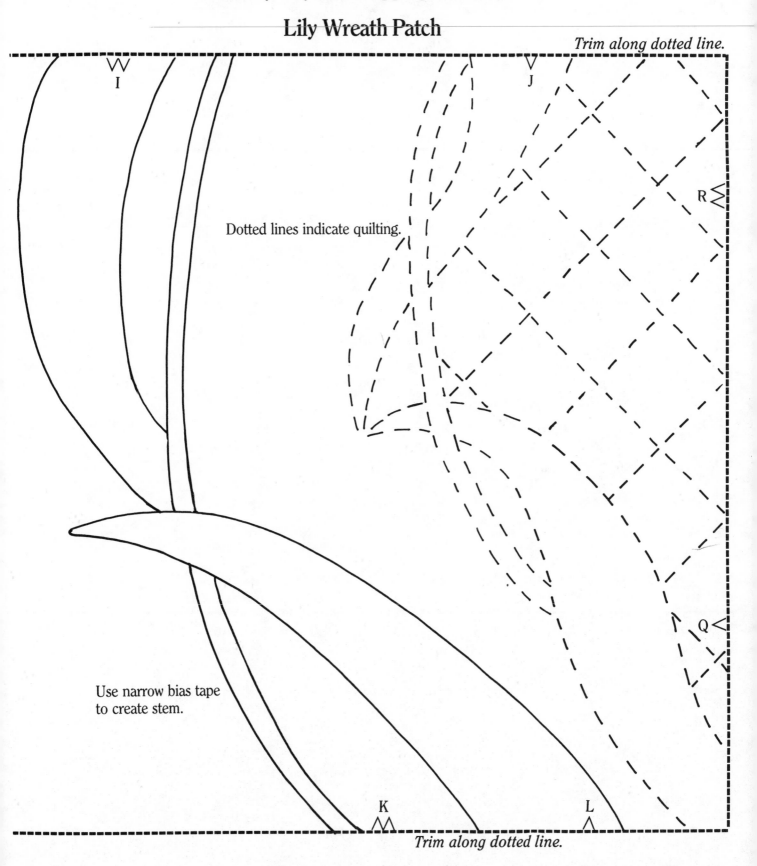

Trim along dotted line.

I

J

Dotted lines indicate quilting.

R

Use narrow bias tape
to create stem.

Q

K

L

Trim along dotted line.

Country Lily Quilt Applique Layout
Leaf Triangle Patch

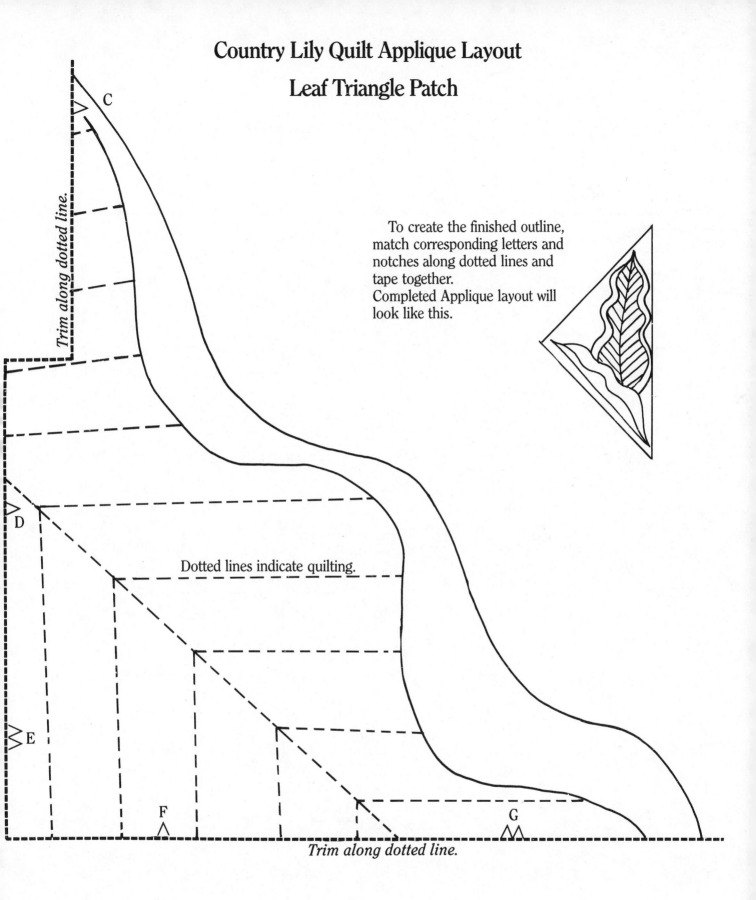

Trim along dotted line.

C

To create the finished outline,
match corresponding letters and
notches along dotted lines and
tape together.
Completed Applique layout will
look like this.

D

Dotted lines indicate quilting.

E

F

G

Trim along dotted line.

Leaf Triangle Patch

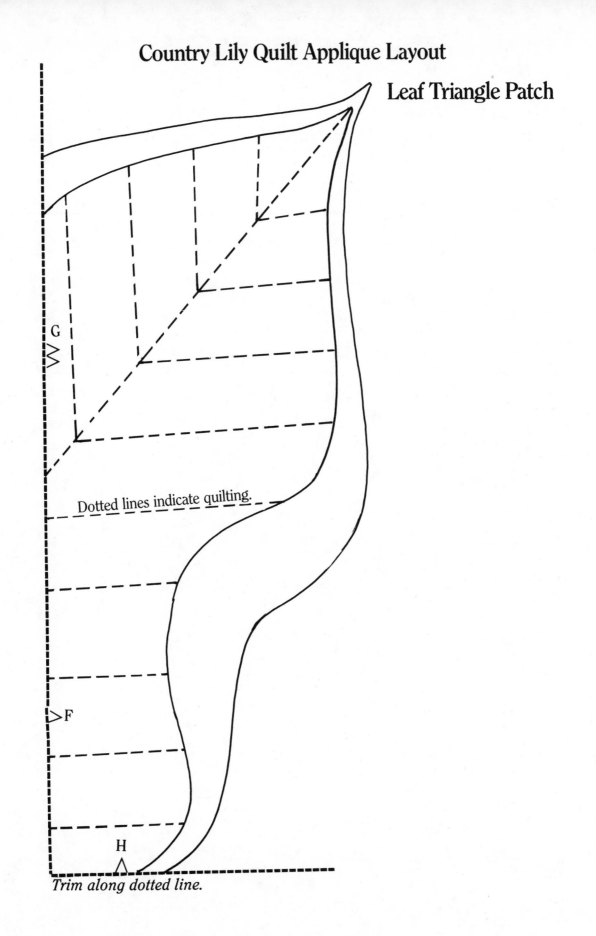

G

Dotted lines indicate quilting.

F

H

Trim along dotted line.

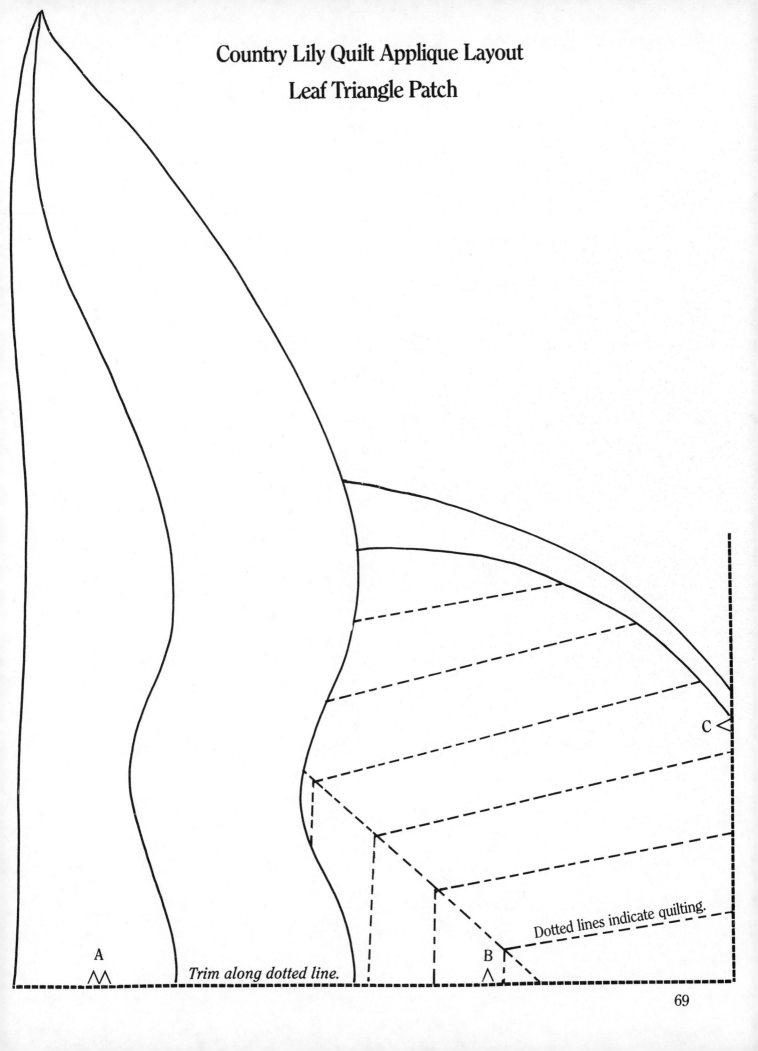

Country Lily Quilt Applique Layout
Leaf Triangle Patch

A

Trim along dotted line.

B

Dotted lines indicate quilting.

C

69

Country Lily Quilt Applique Layout

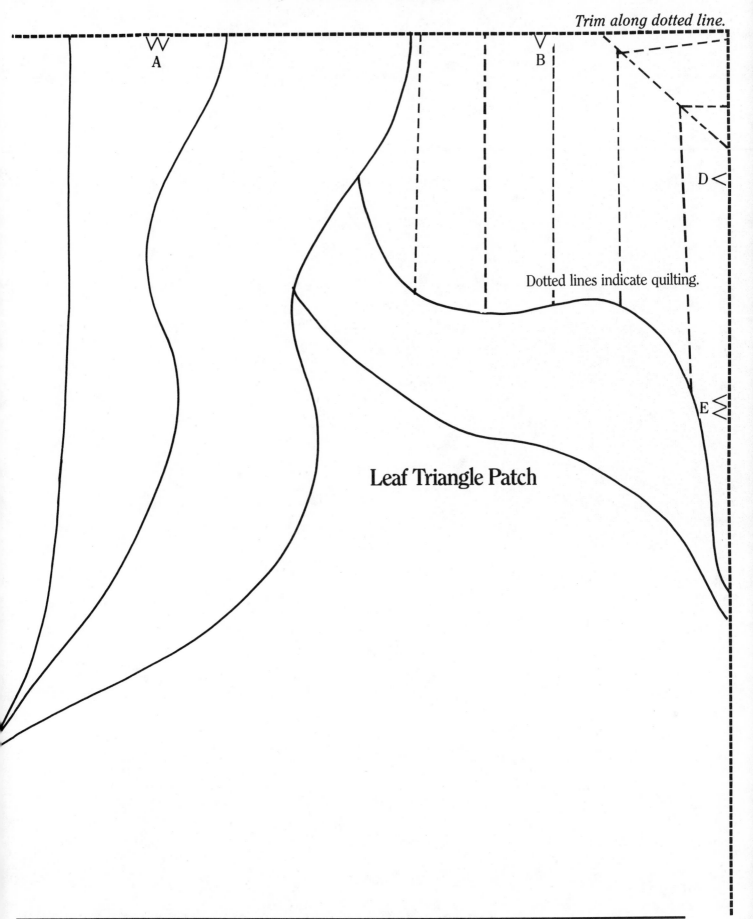

Trim along dotted line.

A

B

Dotted lines indicate quilting.

D

E

Leaf Triangle Patch

Country Lily Quilt Applique Layout
Small Leaf Triangle Patch

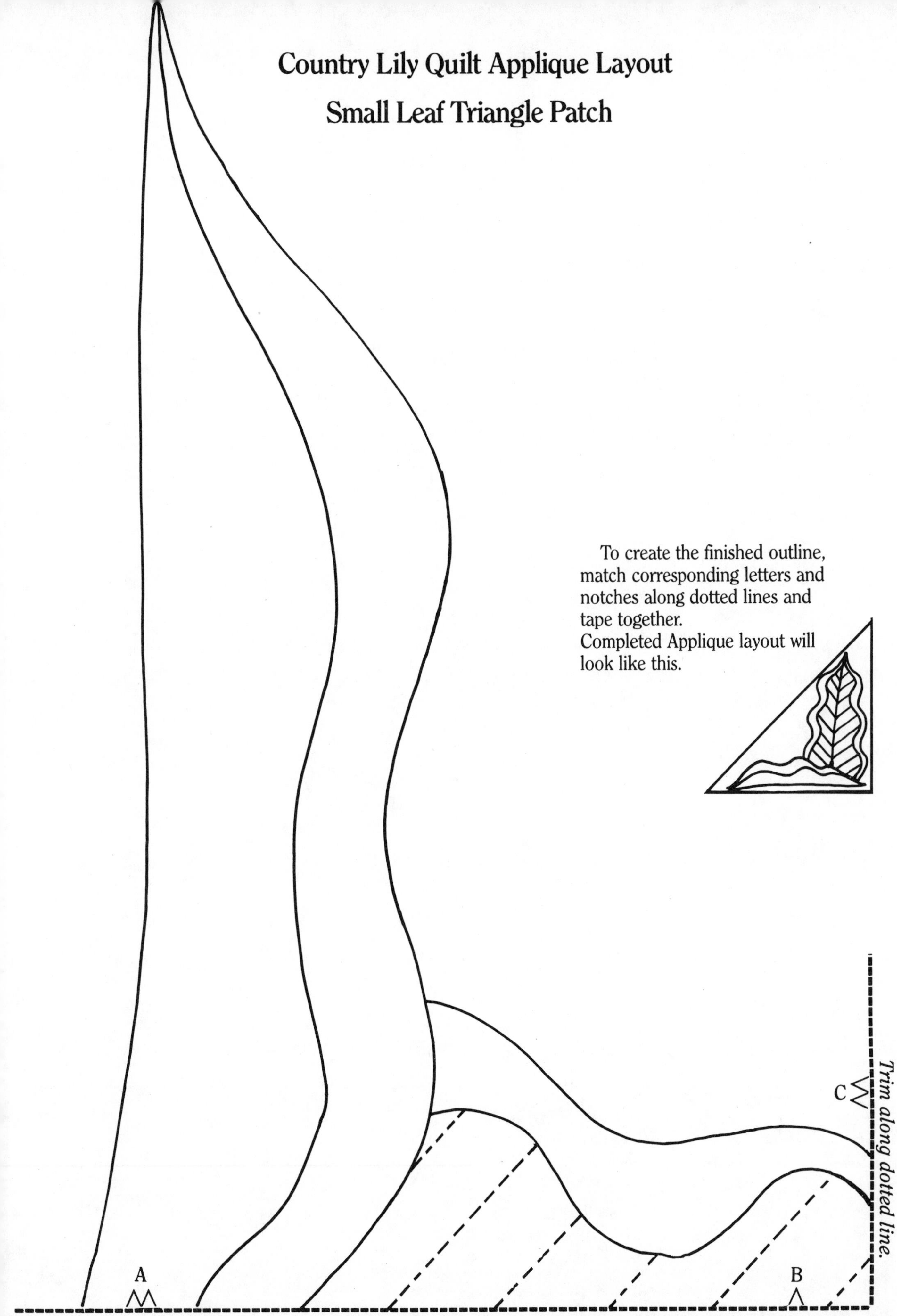

To create the finished outline,
match corresponding letters and
notches along dotted lines and
tape together.
Completed Applique layout will
look like this.

C

Trim along dotted line.

A

B

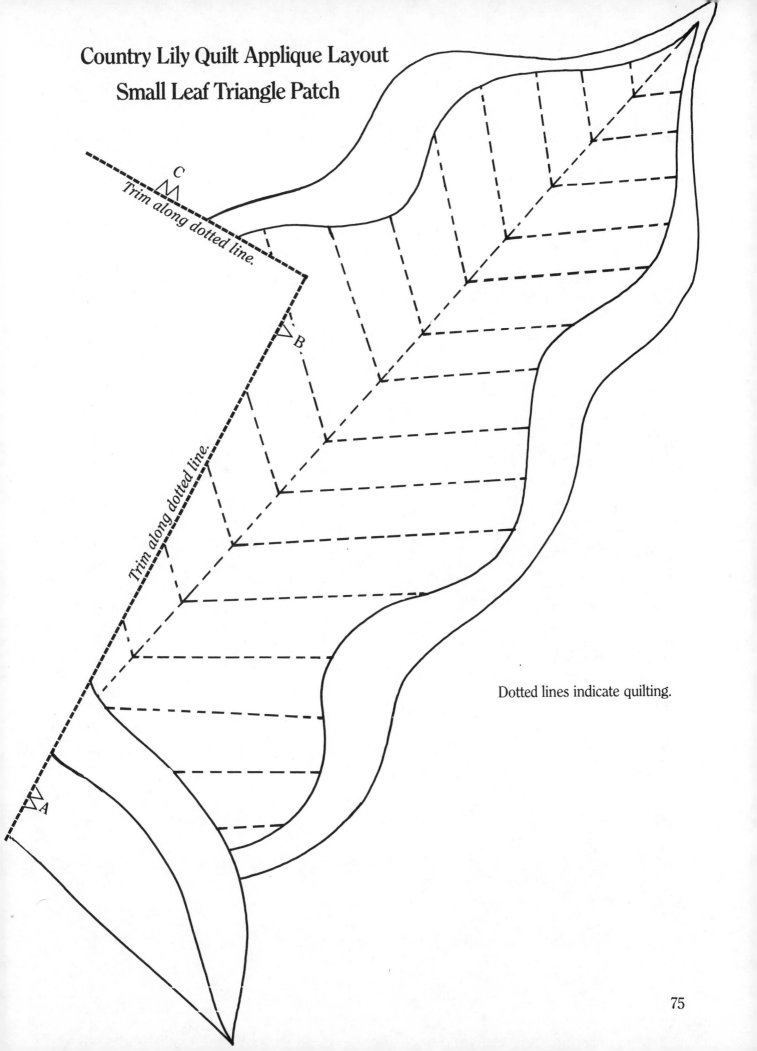

Country Lily Quilt Applique Layout
Small Leaf Triangle Patch

C

Trim along dotted line.

B

Trim along dotted line.

Dotted lines indicate quilting.

A

75

Country Lily Quilt Applique Layout

Side Floral Triangle Patch

To create the finished outline, match corresponding letters and notches along dotted lines and tape together.
Completed Applique layout will look like this.

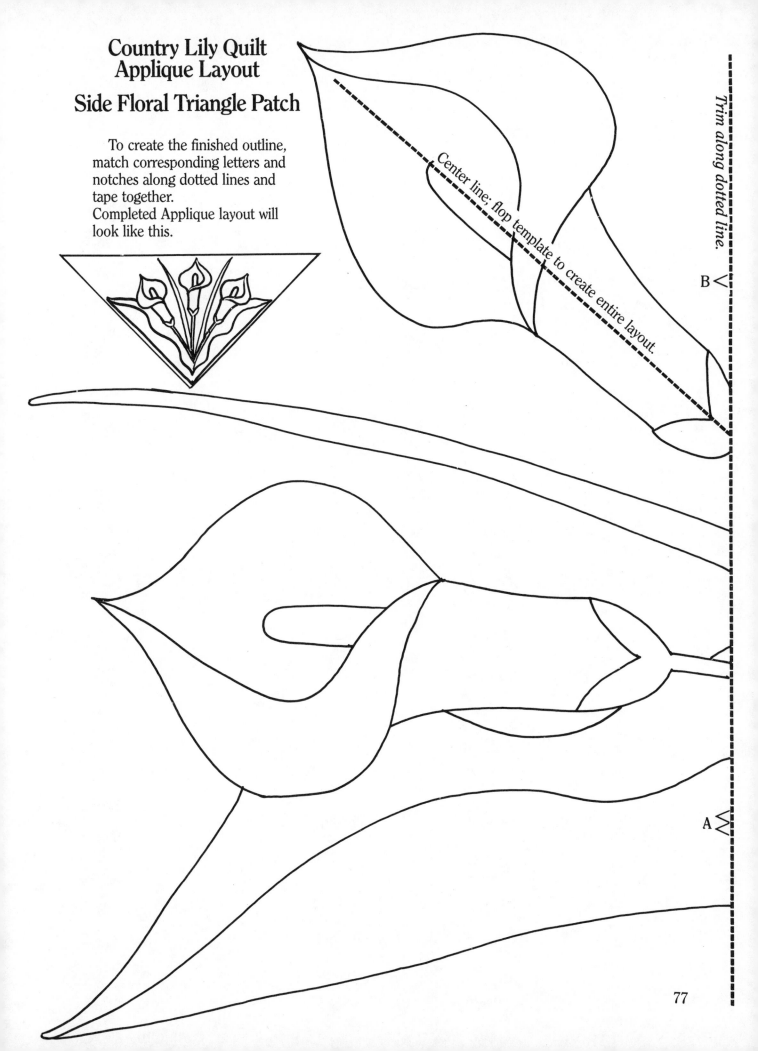

Center line; flop template to create entire layout.

Trim along dotted line.

B

A

77

Country Lily Quilt Applique Layout
Side Floral Triangle Patch

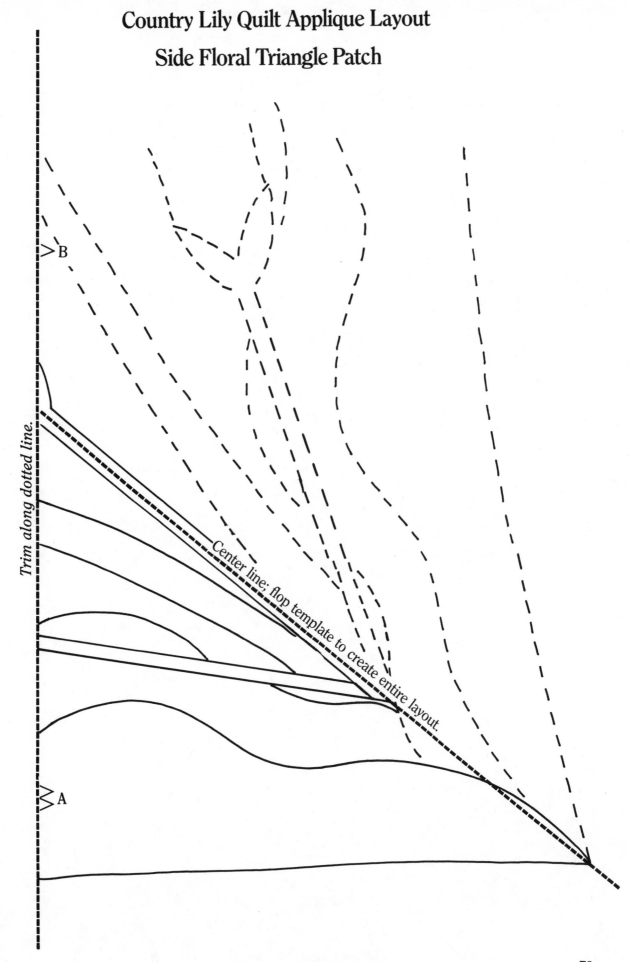

Trim along dotted line.

Center line: flop template to create entire layout.

B

A

79

Country Lily Quilt Quilting Template
Zig-Zag Border

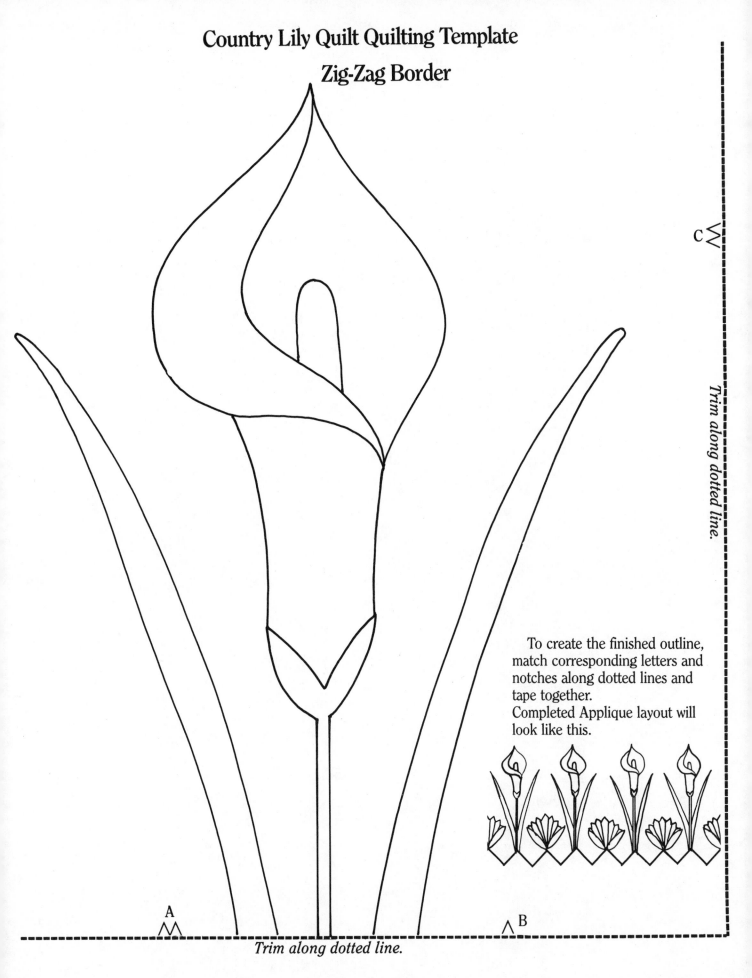

Trim along dotted line.

C

Trim along dotted line.

To create the finished outline, match corresponding letters and notches along dotted lines and tape together.
Completed Applique layout will look like this.

A

B

Country Lily Quilt Quilting Template
Zig-Zag Border .

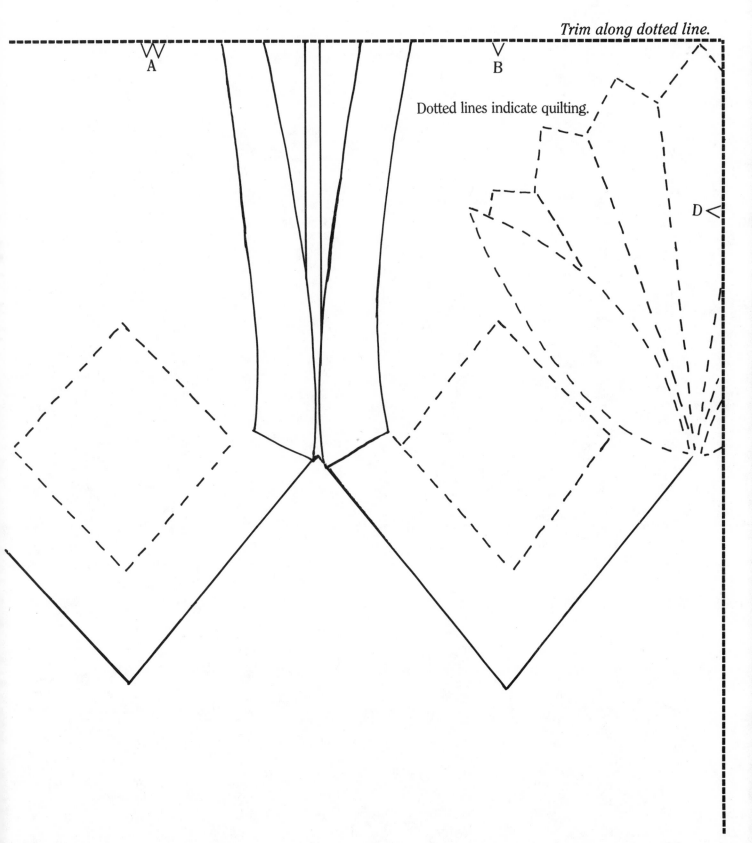

Trim along dotted line.

A

B

Dotted lines indicate quilting.

D

Country Lily Quilt Quilting Template

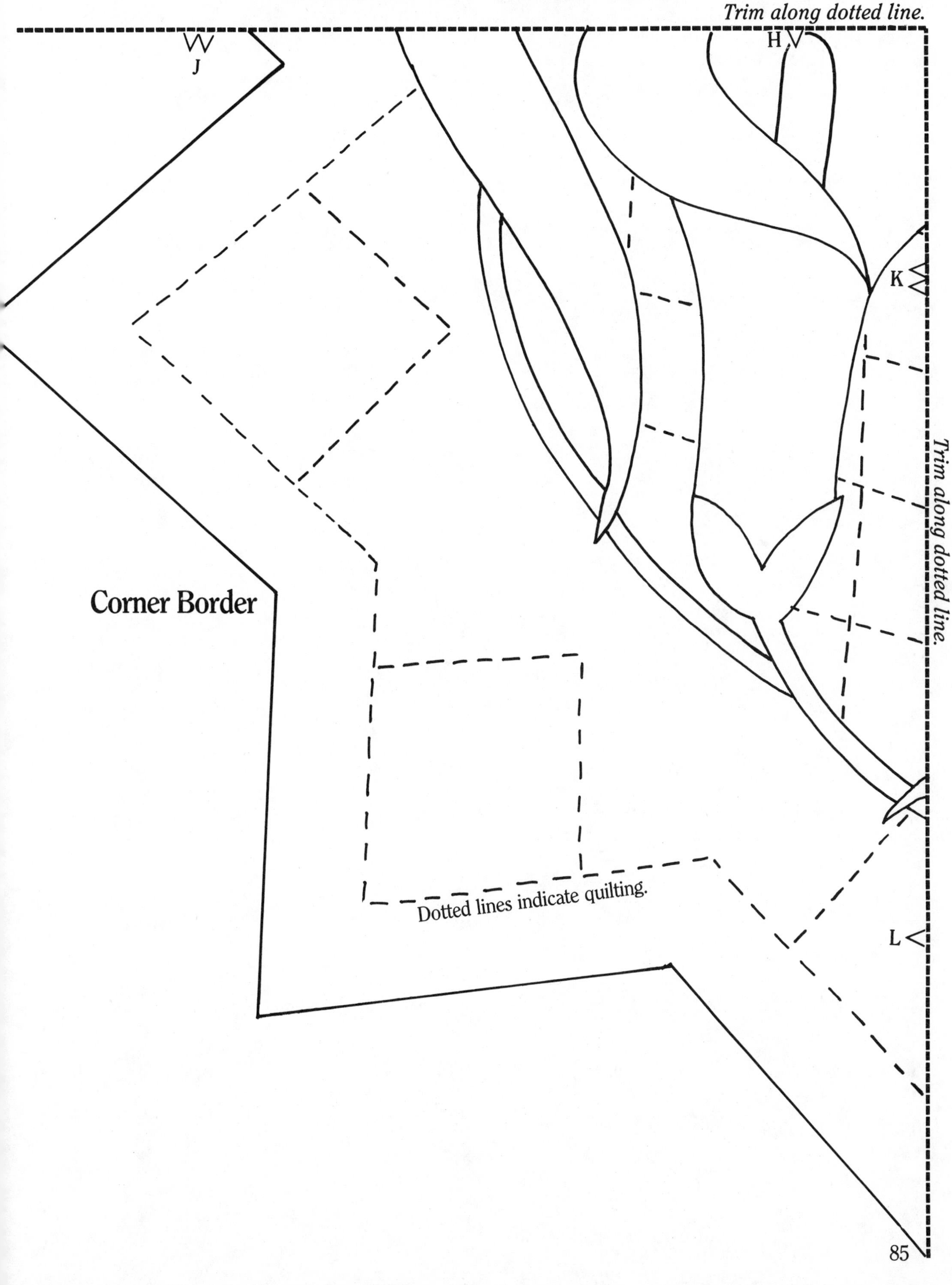

W
J

H ⌄

K

Trim along dotted line.

Corner Border

Dotted lines indicate quilting.

L ⌄

Country Lily Quilt Quilting Template

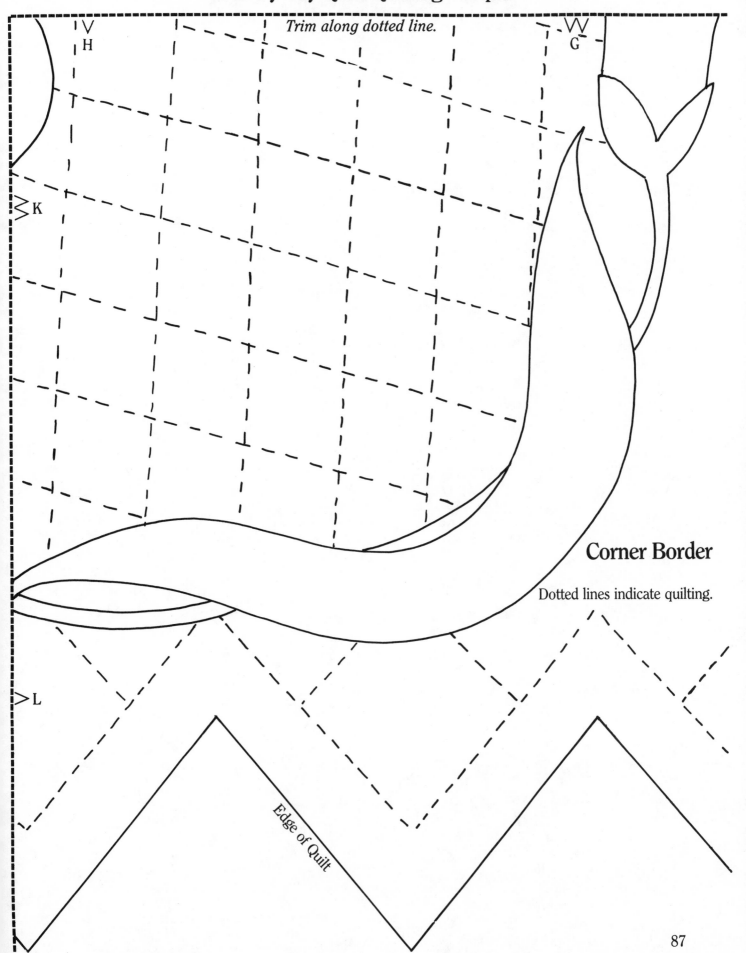

Trim along dotted line.

H

K

Corner Border

Dotted lines indicate quilting.

L

Edge of Quilt

G

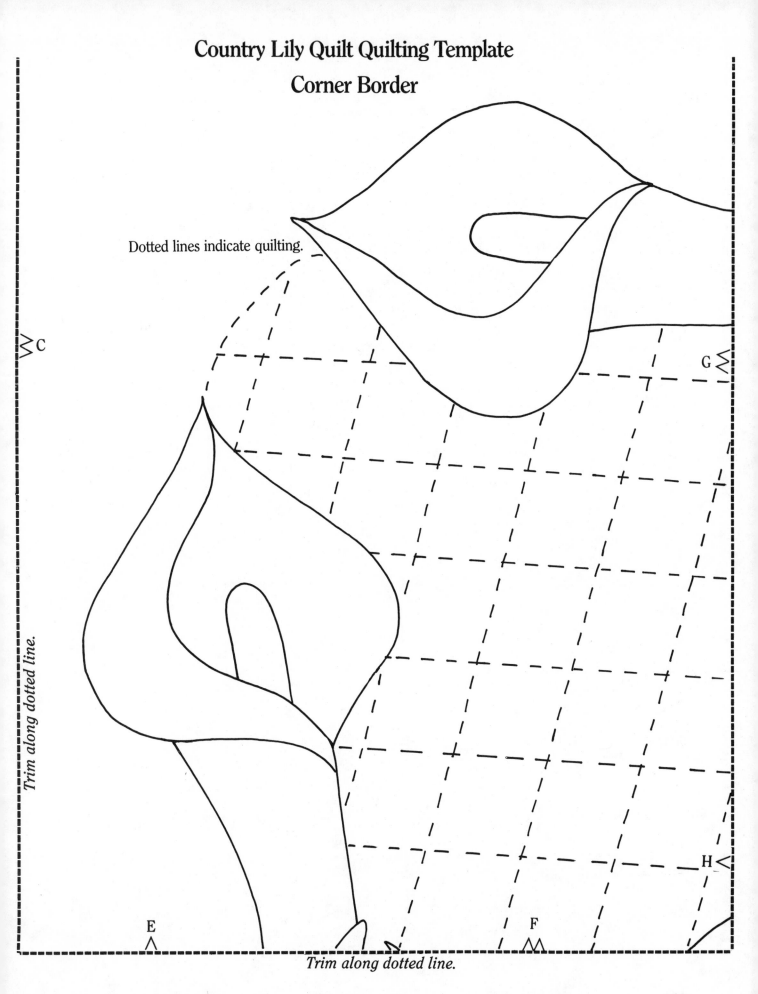

Dotted lines indicate quilting.

Trim along dotted line.

C

G

E

F

H

Trim along dotted line.

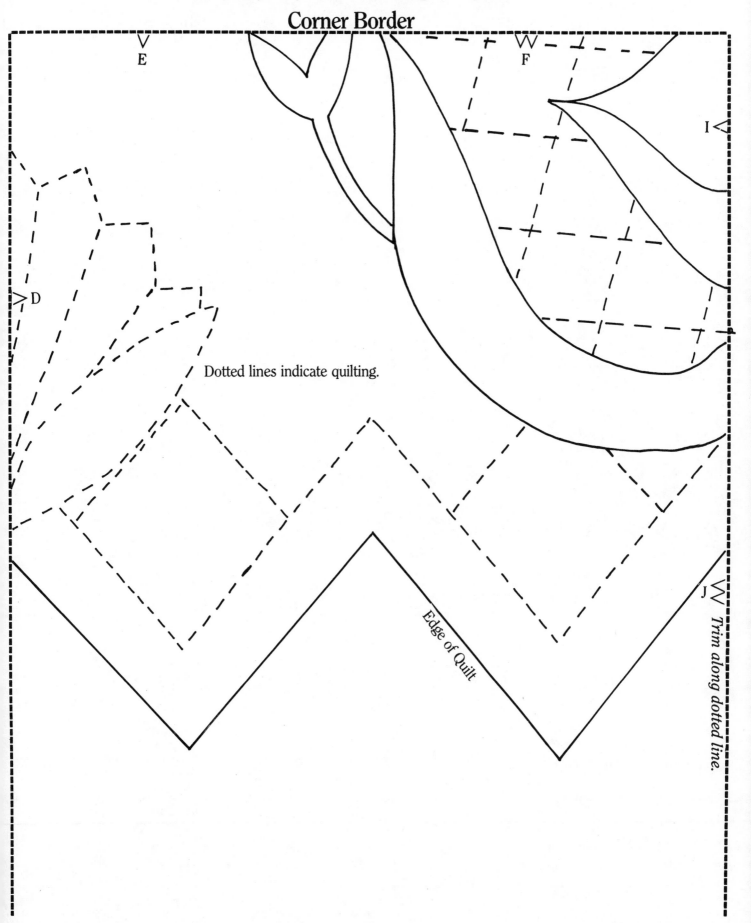

E

W
F

I

D

Dotted lines indicate quilting.

J

Edge of Quilt

Trim along dotted line.

Country Lily Quilt Quilting Template
Zig-Zag Border

Quilted Flower
*(appears on Zig Zag Border
and also along the base
of the Pillow Throw section.)*

Edge of Quilt

Edge of Quilt

The Country Lily Nine-Patch Variation Quilt

The Country Lily Nine-Patch Variation Quilt
Cutting Lay-out for Queen-size or Double-size Quilt

Final size—approximately 96″ x 112″
Measurements include seam allowances

Total yardage for quilt top—9¼ yards
Total yardage for quilt back—6¼ yards
plus 11″ remaining from cutting
borders of quilt top.

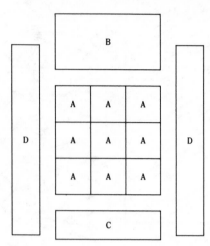

A Patches—cut 9—21½″ square
B Pillow Throw—33″ × 63½″
C Bottom Border—17″ × 63½″
D Side Borders—17″ × 112½″

Quilt Back (6¼ yards) plus 11″ left
from side border section of fabric

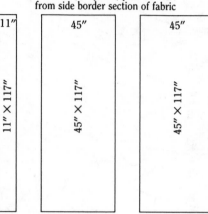

11″	45″	45″
11″ × 117″	45″ × 117″	45″ × 117″

Side Borders (3¼ yards)

Side Border—17″ × 112½″
Side Border—17″ × 112½″
Quilt Back—11″ left

Square Patches, Bottom Border, Pillow Throw (6 yards)

21½″	21½″	21½″	21½″	21½″	
21½″	21½″	21½″	21½″	Bottom Border 17″ × 63½″	Pillow Throw 33″ × 63½″

Assembly Instructions for the Country Lily Nine-Patch
Variation Quilt Queen-size/Double-size

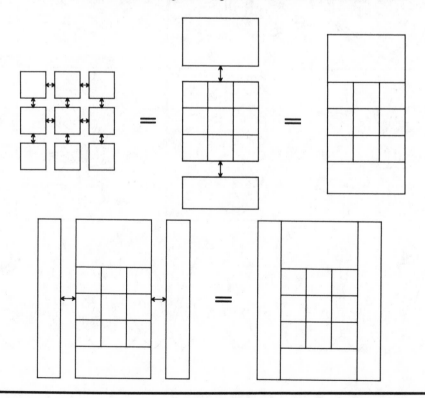

Country Lily Nine-Patch Variation
Quilt Applique Layout

Floral Patch
(for the Country Lily Nine-Patch Variation Quilt)

To create the finished outline, match corresponding letters and notches along dotted lines and tape together.
Completed Applique layout will look like this.

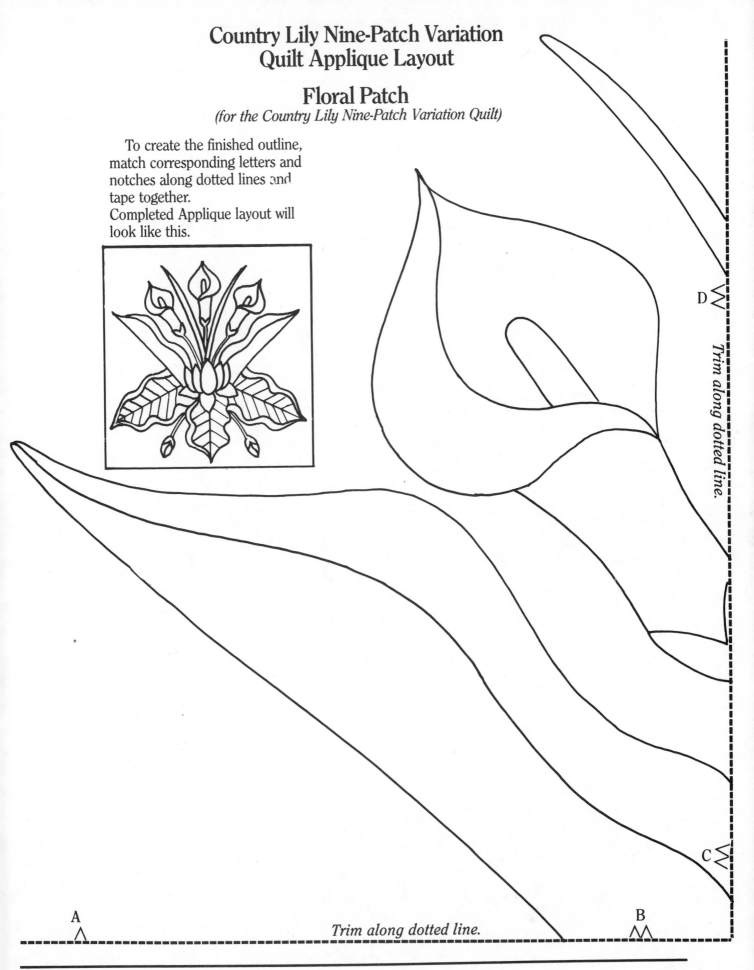

Trim along dotted line.

D

C

A

B

Trim along dotted line.

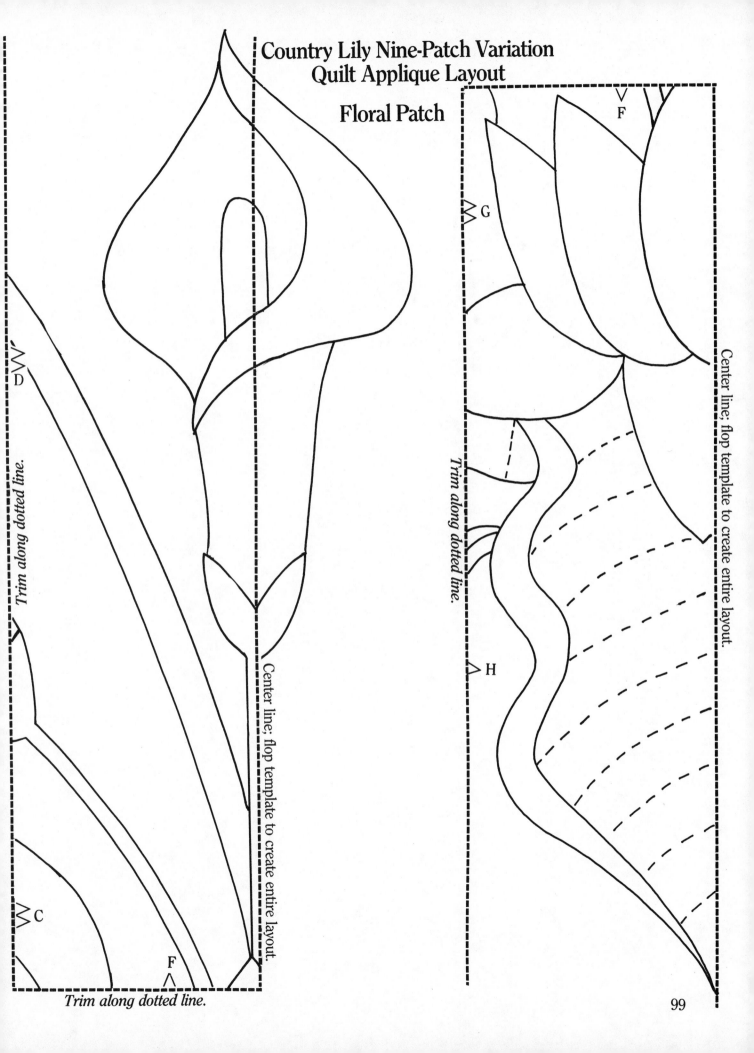

Country Lily Nine-Patch Variation
Quilt Applique Layout

Floral Patch

D

Trim along dotted line.

C

F

Trim along dotted line.

Center line; flop template to create entire layout.

F

G

H

Trim along dotted line.

Center line; flop template to create entire layout.

99

Country Lily Nine-Patch Variation
Quilt Applique Layout

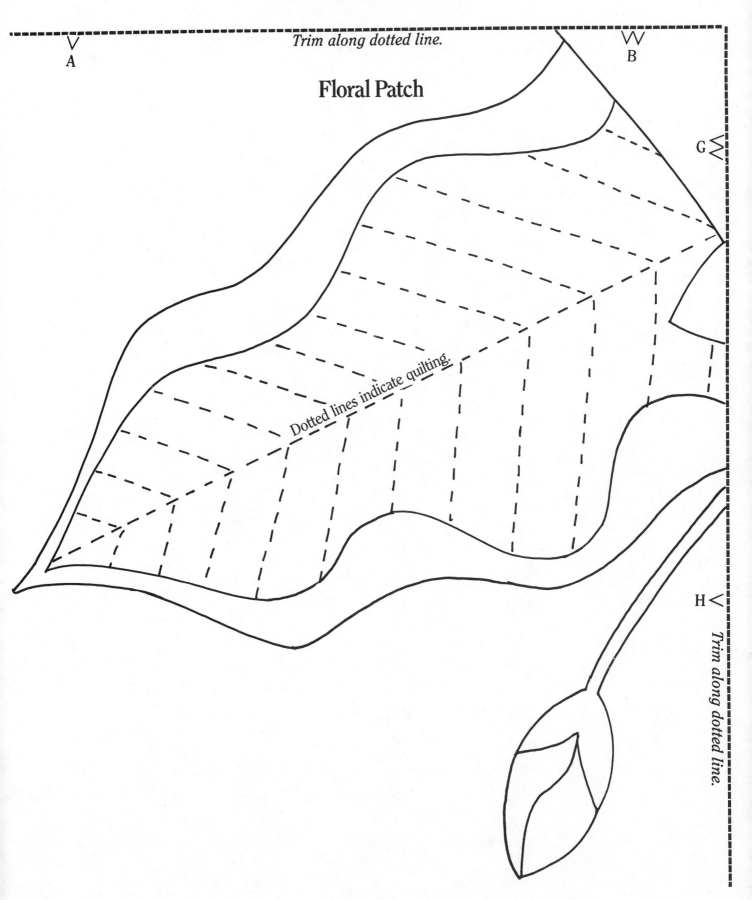

Trim along dotted line.

A

B

G

Floral Patch

Dotted lines indicate quilting.

H

Trim along dotted line.

About The Old Country Store

The People's Place Quilt Museum

Cheryl A. Benner and Rachel T. Pellman are on the staff of The old Country Store, located along Route 340 in Intercourse, Pennsylvania. The store offers crafts from more than 300 artisans, most of whom are local Amish and Mennonites. There are quilts of traditional and contemporary designs, patchwork pillows and pillow kits, afghans, stuffed animals, dolls, tablecloths and Christmas tree ornaments. Other handcrafted items include potholders, sunbonnets and wooden toys.

For the do-it-yourself quilter, the Store offers quilt supplies, fabric at discount prices, and a large selection of quilt books and patterns.

Located on the second floor of the Store is The People's Place Quilt Museum. The Museum, which opened in 1988, features antique Amish quilts and crib quilts as well as a small collection of dolls, doll quilts, socks and other decorative arts.

About The Authors

Cheryl A. Benner and Rachel T. Pellman together developed The Country Lily Quilt and The Country Lily Nine-Patch Variation Quilt. They designed the patterns, then selected fabrics and supervised the making of the original quilts by Lancaster County Mennonite women. This is Benner's and Pellman's second collaboration on a quilt design and book. Their first was the popular *The Country Love Quilt*.

Benner and her husband Lamar live in Honeybrook, Pa. She is a graduate of the Art Institute of Philadelphia (Pa.). Benner is art director for Good Enterprises, Intercourse, Pa.

Pellman lives in Lancaster, Pa., and is manager of The Old Country Store, Intercourse. She is co-author of *The Country Bride Quilt*.

She is the author of *Amish Quilt Patterns* and *Small Amish Quilt Patterns*; co-author with Jan Steffy of *Patterns for Making Amish Dolls and Doll Clothes*; and co-author with her husband, Kenneth, of *The World of Amish Quilts*, *Amish Crib Quilts*, and *Amish Doll Quilts, Dolls, and Other Playthings*.

The Pellmans are the parents of two sons.